"In the wake of the wreckage of the Trump era and pandemic, relief is widespread, but so too is a sense of hopelessness. This book is a call to action, a must-read."

—ROXANNE DUNBAR-ORTIZ, author of
Not "A Nation of Immigrants": Settler Colonialism, White Supremacy, and a History of Erasure and Exclusion

"Many of these remarkable stories from our history will be new to readers—which is sad in a way, since they are important chapters that have been ignored (or erased). But it's a joy in another way, because their fresh power will inspire many to action!"

—BILL MCKIBBEN, author *The End of Nature*

"Filled with inspiring heroes and inspiriting examples, this appeal to make a better world offers an assertive call to seize the time. Combining ethics and idealism with grounded strategies for democratic mobilization, the book presents evocative and compelling guidance about how to organize and identifies ways to communicate without apology."

—IRA KATZNELSON, author of *When Affirmative Action Was White: An Untold History of Racial Inequality in Twentieth-Century America*

"Pondering those who have resisted in our history, Alex Zamalin proposes, is the first step—after COVID and Donald Trump—to making sure that the center and right are not the only forces to reap the benefits of the ongoing American crisis. This is a thrilling read for our times."

—SAMUEL MOYN, Yale University, author of
*Humane: How the United States
Abandoned Peace and Reinvented War*

"If, as Alex Zamalin says, 'radical ideas are most palatable when they're boldly announced and proudly defended in the mainstream,' then this book will be their vehicle. *All Is Not Lost* is a visionary romp through the history we need for a transformational, just, and egalitarian politics. Vivid, inspiring, and accessible, this book gives us heroes who know that 'to change what feels familiar, you have to make a scene.' It should be read by everyone."

—BONNIE HONIG, Brown University, author of
Shell-Shocked: Feminist Criticism After Trump

"In this place of darkness and disaster, Alex Zamalin gives us a guide to overcoming. Written with a great heart and a cool head, he maps what can, what should, be done to build a new world from the shards of the old. This is a call to change within our reach, a map to revolution in the everyday."

—ANNE NORTON, University of Pennsylvania, author of
Leo Strauss and the Politics of American Empire

ALL
IS NOT
LOST

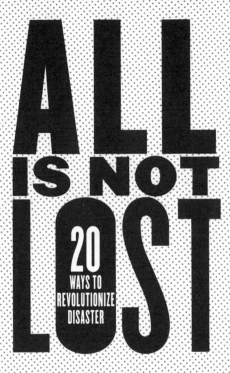

ALL IS NOT LOST

IS NOT

LOST

20 WAYS TO REVOLUTIONIZE DISASTER

ALEX ZAMALIN

BEACON PRESS
BOSTON

BEACON PRESS
Boston, Massachusetts
www.beacon.org

Beacon Press books
are published under the auspices of
the Unitarian Universalist Association of Congregations.

25 24 23 22   8 7 6 5 4 3 2 1

This book is printed on acid-free paper that meets
the uncoated paper ANSI/NISO specifications
for permanence as revised in 1992.

Text design and composition by Kim Arney

Library of Congress Control Number: 2021054429
Paperback ISBN: 978-0-8070-0608-5
Ebook ISBN: 978-0-8070-0609-2

To Alison, Sam, and Anita

CONTENTS

ALL IS NOT LOST

1

DISASTERS ARE OPPORTUNITIES

Disasters are everywhere we look: Climate apocalypse in the form of rising sea levels. Prolonged periods of drought. Tens of thousands of catastrophic wildfires that decimate over eight million acres of forest every year. The novel coronavirus, and its lethal disease COVID-19, killing millions and infecting over one hundred million globally. The rise of far-right white nationalists like Donald Trump in 2016. Terrifying conspiracies like QAnon, which imagine a secret cabal of Democrats and Satanists, "the deep state," working behind the scenes to subvert the Trump administration. Viral videos of Black pain on social media. An unarmed Black man, George Floyd, in Minneapolis is suffocated to death in May 2020 by an officer for eight minutes and forty-six seconds, while pleading for his life and yelling for his deceased mother. In August of the same year in

Kenosha, Wisconsin, another Black man, Jacob Blake, is shot seven times in the back by another cop as he, Blake, approaches his car and reaches into its glove compartment. In 2020, when the COVID pandemic is at its peak, unemployment reaches double digits, disproportionately impacting working-class citizens of color. Millions are without health insurance. There's increased hostility with an existing nuclear power—Russia—and the threat of a new cold war. And a dangerously escalating one with an aspiring global power—Iran.

No wonder disaster makes us want to withdraw. To let the storm pass over us. To wait for brighter days. Disaster makes us paralyzed, forcing us into what is familiar. To embrace what's known. We're debilitated. Critical reflection is gone. We don't want to think about politics. Forget about interests, parties, capitalism, history. Anything, really. It all feels beside the point when you're trying to survive, to avoid doom scrolling through the latest news, ever more horrifying by the day.

Tempting as this pessimism might be, it's not the only response to disaster. And it can't be for those who care about justice. Silence is a boon for inequality. Depression, a victory for mass suffering. Disaster can't control our politics. Nor should it. Especially because when everything appears lost, the battle for the future is waged. Counterintuitive as it may seem, disaster creates unprecedented opportunity to change our world. When all is broken, disoriented, and rearranged—when things collapse, crumble, dissipate, and die and when we need guideposts for something fresh—we can transform society.

Such an opportunity, however, is a double-edged sword. It's good for you but also for anyone who wants to seize it. Especially the powerful. In the aftermath of the 2008 financial crisis, Barack Obama's chief of staff, Rahm Emanuel, would echo a sentiment that became postcard wisdom for policy elites: "You never want a serious crisis to go to waste. I mean, it's an opportunity to do things that you think you could not do before."[1] A senior advisor to Bill Clinton in 1993, member of the US House of Representatives from the Fifth Congressional District of Illinois, and Democratic mayor of Chicago from 2011 to 2019, Emanuel has, throughout his career, used disaster to institute his centrism. He talked Obama out of demanding a public option for his signature policy, the Affordable Care Act, in 2010 as a way to keep the healthcare industry happy and not alienate suburban white voters. As Chicago mayor, Emanuel was responsible for the largest closure of public schools— fifty—to offset the city's budget deficits.

In August 2020, as COVID was rapidly changing the world as we knew it, he gave the Democratic presidential candidate, Joe Biden, a bit of advice on CNBC: "Two things I would say if I was advising an administration," Emanuel said. "One is there's no new Green Deal, [and] there's no Medicare for All, probably the single two topics that were discussed the most."[2] Indeed, rather than transform American policy in this chaotic moment, Emanuel proposed that nominee Biden use the unmitigated moral disaster of the Trump presidency to change the composition of the Democratic Party's electorate, to bring aboard as many moderate Republicans as possible. "This will be the year of the Biden Republican," Emanuel declares. "My view is you don't want this to be a transactional election. You want this to be the opportunity of a transformational election."

Emanuel's views should anger progressives. Why leverage disaster to expand the influence of the Right, rather than transform radically unequal institutions? But Emanuel's thinking isn't new. It's been a staple of reactionary thought for decades. In his 1982 preface to the fortieth-anniversary rerelease of his classic book *Capitalism and Freedom*, the libertarian economist Milton Friedman famously asserted, "Only a crisis—actual or perceived—produces real change. When that crisis occurs, the actions that are taken depend on the ideas that are lying around. . . . Our basic function [is] to develop alternatives to existing policies, to keep them alive and available until the politically impossible."[3] Friedman, who first published his book in 1962, couldn't imagine how successful this approach would be from the 1970s onward. Right-wing disruption common to what we now call the "neoliberal era" of government—to cut public programs, deregulate the banking industry, eliminate the social welfare state, privatize public schools and prisons, crush public- and private-sector unions—has defined the last four decades.

If Rahm Emanuel had his way, we would extend this neoliberal era indefinitely. After COVID-19 left many retail stores shuttered and their employees subsequently unemployed, our prophet of disaster took to the airways once more to offer sage advice to the incoming Biden administration. "There's going to be people like at JCPenney and other retail—those jobs aren't coming back. Give them the tools," Emanuel said. "Six months, you're going to become a computer coder. We'll pay for it. . . . We need to give them a lifeline to what's the next chapter."[4] Job retraining programs. Not unionizing Amazon workers. Coding courses, not a living wage. Jeff Bezos couldn't have found a better paid spokesperson.

To be fair, Emanuel is right. But not in the way he thinks. Disaster *is* an opportunity to change the world. This is the first lesson of this book. You can expand democracy for the majority in times of crisis. Luckily for us, there's a rich history of activists, intellectuals, and artists navigating the treacherous terrain of the unknown and unseen, and living to tell their stories in a new world they both helped create and, at times, never thought would be possible.

They're the best disrupters of disasters in US history. Not the ones Silicon Valley has in mind. They're not rich. Or powerful. They often don't have the ears of presidents and CEOs. And their stories are missing from history books: Indigenous people, poor people, the enslaved, utopians, pacifists, antiwar activists, Black freedom fighters, feminists, queer citizens, hippies, and environmentalists. But they're the ones who give us the hope so urgently needed today. From them, you'll learn how to resist successfully, speak emphatically, organize collectively, memorialize ethically, dream poetically, write prophetically, occupy vigorously, build durably, and act decisively.

Many of the college students I teach know very little about these figures. If they do know something about them, it's romanticized. You know the tired narrative.

Once upon a time in the 1960s, there were courageous activists who cared about things fighting for a better world. Now everyone is on social media, crafting the perfect image of themselves, too apathetic about injustice, too cynical to care. Every disaster, my students think, is unprecedented. We can't do anything about it, even if we tried. Every year we have these same conversations in class. Like clockwork.

But if my students knew history, this history I see played out yearly wouldn't repeat.

The activists you meet in these pages have suffered from the same anxieties you do. Were told to grow up. To get a job. To get off the street. Perhaps, deep down, my students know they aren't so dissimilar from the activists who came before them. But they are afraid to admit it. Because if they did, then they'd recognize that they have a choice to start anew.

Hope. The concept may seem old-fashioned. Or it may be the last thing you feel when you're living through disaster. But hope is the force behind a revolutionary life. Hope motivates you to confront the abyss in the face of long odds and impossible obstacles. This isn't wishful thinking. Not the innocent kind you see in children's books. It's the hope you feel in the dark. You can't see a better future. You don't know if you'll arrive there, ever. You question your intuitions. You're shaken by your doubts. But without hope, there's no way out of disaster. Without hope, this disaster—and the next one, and the one after that—will swallow you and everything you hold dear. Hope is like love. You feel grounded in the world. But petrified of making yourself vulnerable by putting yourself out there.

Insist that democracy is, in fact, possible in America, that capitalism won't rule forever, that climate catastrophe will be addressed in radical ways, that labor will have dignity, that gender identity will be honored. Democracy is as radical as it is necessary. It requires courage. Endless amounts. But if there's anything the stories chronicled here offer, it's that democracy, like the hope and love that nourish it, can't ever be abandoned. Not now. Not ever.

2

RESIST

Disaster crushes the spirit. It sets the stage for political disengagement. When you're crushed, it's hard to get involved. To show up. You saw this after Donald Trump was elected in November 2016, on a platform of naked racism and aspirational authoritarianism. Within his first year in office, Trump's demonizing rhetoric and destabilizing narcissism led to an epidemic of nihilism: 36 percent of US adults described feeling more anxious in 2017 than they did the previous year, and 25 percent of Americans reported having more trouble forging closer connections with loved ones. One psychologist, Jennifer Panning, termed this the "Trump Anxiety Disorder," which she defined as "increased worry, obsessive thought patterns, muscle tension and obsessive preoccupation with the news."[1]

Even as Trump's presidency was coming to a close in September 2020, some, like the writer Mychal Denzel

Smith in the *New York Times*, openly wondered whether the four years of Trump, as well as witnessing the wildfires in California, an emboldened ICE (Immigration and Customs Enforcement), and the loss of hundreds of thousands of precious Americans to COVID-19, had left an irreversible mark: "I had come around to believing that a slow, frustrating but ultimately sustainable victory and all the jubilation that would come along with it was something my friends' children might someday experience. That sense of possibility has largely dissipated."[2] Smith's feeling is relatable, but energetic mobilization is essential. Why? When defiance is missing during a crisis, coercive authority benefits most. Then, the powerful ruthlessly sink their teeth into society and amplify the pain they've already caused.

Despair needn't create paralysis. To the contrary, it can motivate you to risk everything, to find courage wherever you can, to trust the democratic resources available to you, and to never back down. Power can be forged among the dispossessed. Solidarity can be found in the darkest of places. Always resist and make resistance into a tradition. It will inspire you. And those who come after.

US history begins this way. Indigenous communities—the Muskogee, Chickasaw, and Choctaw Nations in the South, and the Wampanoag, Pequot, and Narragansett in New England—did whatever they could to protect their communities from being eviscerated without the means of germ warfare or high-grade weaponry deployed by European settlers in their genocidal campaigns.

What Indigenous citizens faced is unimaginable. Every time you gather around the Thanksgiving table, remember the bloody origins of American empire. In August 1609, the military man John Smith, who has been lionized in children's books through the Pocahontas myth, demanded food from Powhatan Confederacy farmers. After they refused, Smith unleashed a war of extermination that lasted one year. Gruesome spectacles of violence are morally reprehensible. But they also have a political function, which is to remind you that powerful people will stop at nothing to realize what they want and impose their will upon you. The rules don't apply to them; there's no limit to their madness. In July 1636, the Plymouth Colony, led by John Mason, decided that, although their introduction of smallpox had wiped out a large portion of the Pequot fishing community there, it was time to slaughter Indigenous women and children, and burn everything in sight. To encourage private bounty hunters to earn their paychecks, New

Englanders pioneered scalping. In 1645, the Tidewater War saw Virginia settlers starve out Indigenous villages. The Indigenous population, which once stood at one hundred million, had dwindled to ten million after the pandemic of colonization began.

Against this backdrop, Indigenous people resisted. The Powhatans attacked a Virginia colony in 1622. In New England, the Pequot defended the 250 square miles of their territory from 1636 to 1637, and the Wampanoag used guerrilla tactics to lay siege to settler encampments in sporadic battles during what came to be known as King Philip's War from 1675 to 1676.

But even more significant than armed struggle in defending Indigenous communities were their complex systems of government, an alternative to the insatiable individualism of European settlers who saw Indigenous land as property to be confiscated. Sovereign nations east of the Mississippi ruled through a council of elders that represented various lineages in a community. The Haudenosaunee Constitution emphasized peace and justice. Treaties between different nations were deemed sacred and inviolable.[3] The Iroquois had an advanced moral code, which demanded that those who stole food change their behavior—only then would they be readmitted to the community. Women Iroquois elders selected and could remove male elders who violated their fiduciary responsibility to protect the collective's interest.[4]

Imagine if these traditions informed our politics. Politicians wouldn't be laughing all the way to the bank, enriched by powerful lobbying groups. Mutual aid would take the place of ruthless competition. Restorative justice would be practiced over mass incarceration.

During colonial America, enslaved African Americans were aware of Indigenous resistance. Ever since the first twenty people were kidnapped from western Africa and brought to Jamestown, Virginia, in 1619, rebellion had permeated the southern plantation. Africans in Virginia, North Carolina, South Carolina, and Maryland poisoned their masters, feigned ignorance, went on strike, exchanged gossip, and sabotaged the machines they worked on. Scores escaped with nothing but their freedom—by foot, in water, through thickets, in the dead of night, naked, hungry, with fierce determination and faith. Many of these fugitives, known as Maroons, left in groups and found safe haven in the forests of Virginia and the swamps of Georgia. Among the most notable are the Great Dismal Swamp between North Carolina and Virginia, in which thousands lived, and a settlement in Bas du Fleuve, Louisiana.

Because Maroon colonies existed outside recorded history, we know little about them, but what we do know gives us a glimpse into how to create a community during crisis. In 1724, a Maroon named Cesar lived in a forest close to several plantations on the Eastern Shore of Virginia, where a free Black couple gave him food and an enslaved one gave him shelter. Solidarity traversed the color line. Cesar bartered berries he had harvested for cornmeal with two white women, who gave him a bed to sleep in their home.

Fugitives joined up, living in the borderlands. Their very existence emboldened others to do the same. In March 1710, in Virginia, a group of enslaved colonial-born African Americans, Indians, and newly arrived African men conspired to escape bondage. But slave-holders crushed this plot before it unfolded, and the accused were hanged and decapitated. Yet slaveholder fury was betrayed by crippling anxiety. This rising tide of defiance was an existential threat. In 1721, the Virginia colonial governor Alexander Spotswood worried about a small group of runaways in the Blue Ridge Mountains, who lived adjacent to a frontier settlement occupied by poor whites. What would happen if interracial coalitions formed? The architects of the racist-settler complex didn't want to know, for good reason.

Outside the official record of monumental events is where ordinary people gather, talk, laugh, and organize. This is where liberation unfolds and the roots of resistance flourish. You won't find militant manifestos or polished philosophical treatises here. You'll see secret meetings in cramped apartments where fast-food workers organize to unionize, despite the threat of retaliation from multinational corporations. This is where intersectional feminists in church basements debate how to pressure their local community to build affordable housing, and where anti-racists in school gyms devise tactics for defunding the police. You'll find surprising connections. The sharing of experiences. And the breaking of bread. Recognition of collective responsibility and interconnected fate. Statues won't be erected, and street corners won't be renamed to commemorate these heroes. True. But without them, democracy doesn't survive. Not after this disaster, or the next.

TAKE BACK THE STREETS

Public space is the arena of democracy. When crisis strikes, you look out the window to see what's happening outside. That's because whoever controls the streets often controls the narrative. When you see armored vehicles and riot squads equipped with military-grade armor that is designed for the battlefield in Iraq and Afghanistan roaming Los Angeles, Kenosha, Minneapolis, or Chicago on a summer night in 2020, you know the state is flexing its muscle.

That's also why Trump unleashed the force of the DC police, who pushed out nonviolent anti-racist protesters denouncing the murder of George Floyd with suffocating tear gas on Lafayette Square. Why did Trump stroll down from his residence at 1600 Pennsylvania Avenue at 7 p.m. on June 1, 2020, and pose for a five-minute photo-op with a Bible in his right hand at St.

John's Episcopal Church? He wanted to say: "I represent the people." But when protesters—chanting, shouting, singing, dancing—showed up with signs, they contested his dubious assertion.

Look closely at Trump as he's posing before the cameras at St. John's Church. Notice his palpable unease. The strain in his face, distorted with apprehension. The discomfort in his movements, as he fidgets with the Bible and then mechanically raises it skyward in his right hand. He betrays the image of strength he so desperately wants to project.

The aspiring authoritarian is afraid of something he goes to great lengths to hide from you: whoever is more convincing in representing the will of people is likely to persuade them that they, are, in fact, their representative. As a citizen, you don't have tanks. You can't call the military. But when it comes to gaining popular support for your cause, you have an advantage: you're not paid; this isn't your job. You might lose your job when you show up, but you're doing it because you can't stay home. You'll make your voice known. Occupy the streets and make them yours. It will go viral.

Pre-Revolutionary America is filled with examples of people seizing the streets to protest the crisis of economic

inequality. During November 1747, a three-day uprising
in Boston, known as the Knowles Riot, saw ordinary
people capture several British naval officers and a dep-
uty in response to the mandatory conscription, known
as impressment, of forty-six men into naval service by
British admiral Charles Knowles. Twelve years later,
there was the revolt against the Stamp Act of 1765, when
a group of sailors raided the home of Charleston trader
Henry Laurens, who was believed to hold the stamped
paper everyone was forced to buy to raise revenue for
the British Crown. In 1772, sixty men—farmers, sailors,
and merchants—came out of eight boats and burned to
the ground the British merchant ship, the *Gaspee*, after
it ran aground in Warwick Bay in Rhode Island, where
it had been in hot pursuit of a colonial ship that was sus-
pected of illicit trade.[1]

Public scenes leave a lasting imprint. The Knowles
Riot made quite the impression upon a young man
named Samuel Adams Jr. of Massachusetts, a privileged
scion of a well-to-do businessman and politician, who
had just finished his master's degree at Harvard University. So deeply affected was Adams by these rebels that
it inspired his faith in the idea that liberty is an unques-
tioned right and that human rights must be defended

without qualification. But it's hard to police something that doesn't recognize the authority of the police, that marches to the beat of its own drum. The Revolutionary War veteran Daniel Shays descended upon Western Massachusetts in 1787 with a band of four thousand men because they couldn't survive crippling debt. Upon hearing the news of Shays's insurrection, Sam Adams was aghast. What had become of Adams's earlier enthusiasm for democratic insurrection? Now, reaping benefits as a member of the ruling class, Adams wrote the Massachusetts Riot Act of 1786, which gave license to armed militias to stamp out popular revolt. Several years later, Adams endorsed the suppression of what came to be known as the Whiskey Rebellion of 1794, started by poor farmers who resisted efforts at federal tax collection.[2]

Privately, Thomas Jefferson, unlike Adams, knew better than to disparage radical dissent with an egalitarian purpose. Democracy can't survive without it. In a letter to Abigail Adams—wife of John Adams, Sam's second cousin—Jefferson, away in France as the US ambassador, quipped, "I like a little rebellion now and again. . . . It is like a storm in the atmosphere."[3] Jefferson's magnum opus, the Declaration of Independence, justifies the very nature of democratic populism—of enslaved revolt, Indigenous rebellion, poor people's movements, feminist uprisings—of making your aspirations known. The Declaration steals the right of creating government from kings and God. It places it in your hands to reason whether democratic revolution, which is a right, is advisable or not. It inaugurates the push and pull of debate and disagreement that characterizes living together. It brings you into the fold with others, even if your voice isn't heard.

Unfortunately, Jefferson betrayed the Declaration of Independence. As a gentleman of aristocratic birth from Virginia—a planter's son, the third of ten children—he owned over one hundred slaves, and after his death, only two were freed from his plantation, Monticello, "little mountain." As the third US president, Jefferson extended US imperialism through the Louisiana Purchase in 1803, when his administration bought 827,000 acres west of the Mississippi River for $15 million, wreaking havoc on Indigenous people. He had a long relationship and fathered children with one of the enslaved women at Monticello, Sally Hemings, who legally couldn't say no to any of his advances.

But Jefferson's reactionary behavior can't repress the revolutionary spirit of the Declaration. You see it being reborn every time citizens take back the streets. When graffiti artists paint gorgeous murals on sidewalks declaring in large block letters "Black Lives Matter" after the murder of Breonna Taylor in 2020. It's present when interracial youth defiantly sing "You About to Lose Yo Job"—a rap anthem that became a sensation during the Black Lives Matter summer 2020 protests after a Black woman, Johnniqua Charles, issued a stern warning to a security officer in South Carolina arresting her as she tried to reenter a strip club to reclaim her purse. "Why are you detaining me?" Charles asks him. When he doesn't respond, she declares, "You about to lose your job."[4] You also see the Declaration's revolutionary spirit when DACA recipients—undocumented citizens who were brought to the US as children—come out of the shadows in Arizona and Texas, agitating for full rights given to birthright citizens.

The street is seized and so, too, is the meaning of who belongs in America and what America is. Make politicians respond to public spectacles. Otherwise, they'll continue to read the public opinion polls, which only prop up the million-dollar political consulting industry. Opinion polls offer a tiny snapshot of what the majority wants. "The people" is what you say it is. Keep up the pressure. Imagine how different things would be if protests became parades of resistance on a daily basis, lasting not for days but for months or years? Imagine what would happen if the city square became a stage for forging a new national identity and a new language of belonging? It would be stunning.

4

PATRIOTISM ISN'T THE ANSWER

The warm comfort of home is a perfect narcotic for the anxiety that arrives after disaster. When you're unmoored from your roots, a sense of belonging to a community makes you feel grounded. Remember the bipartisan support of US troops when they were sent to Iraq by the George W. Bush administration to shock Saddam Hussein into submission in March 2003. Recall the invocation for national unity after Americans watched in horror as white supremacists, equipped with tiki torches and guns, chanting into the summer night "Jews will not replace us!," descended upon Charlottesville, Virginia, in August 2017. Think about the suburban neighborhoods where white, college-educated, affluent voters hang American flags on their white porches. They were a core constituency for the electoral coalition of Joe Biden, whose winning presidential campaign slogan against the undemocratic authoritarianism of Trump in 2020 was to "redeem the soul of the nation." But patriotism is the last thing we need to stitch up our wounds. Patriotism is a dangerous anesthetic. It prevents us from knowing where or what our wounds are, and how exactly they ought to be treated. Patriotism establishes a community of us against them, where angels and demons are what we see instead of smart or bad policies. When the nation becomes what you profess undying allegiance toward, criticism is impossible.

Don't be unflinchingly patriotic. Distrust anyone who declares that America is great no matter how many examples of the nation's supremacy that they give. There's a lot they're hiding that they would rather ignore. Instead, make the nation bend to your loving example. Become an iconoclast. Ruthless skepticism pierces the piety of exceptionalism. Live a moral life that goes against what you'll be told is sacred.

The Quaker John Woolman, born in Burlington, New Jersey, in 1720, thought he would forever remain an upstanding entrepreneur in the colonial American community where he sold sugar, rum, and pork at reasonable prices in a local shop. Much to his own surprise, Woolman became a revolutionary. The catastrophe that shook him wide awake was the French and Indian War, or what later became known as the Seven Years' War (1756–1763). Woolman was stunned to hear some of his Quaker brethren who controlled the Pennsylvania legislature and whose faith commanded pacifism come out in defense of levying taxes on colonial subjects to support Britain in the conflict.

They did this, even though the news from the battlefront was terrifying. Thousands died in the battle between the two superpowers. Violence spread like wildfire throughout the colonies. The British, led by General Jeffrey Amherst, in 1760 shamelessly targeted Cherokee noncombatants in Virginia, children and women. They were enthusiastically helped by American settlers, who used scalping, pillaging, and theft to instill as much terror as possible in the Indigenous community. There were the "Paxton Boys," a group of fifty Ulster-Scot vigilantes from Pennsylvania who, unprovoked, in December 1763 marched to a Susquehannock settlement, where they slaughtered six men and burned their homes.

Most Americans don't protest war—and they didn't back then—and this silence has consequences. When you don't say anything, government can better continue its lethal policies. Remember that government relies on consent, so it begins to crumble when you say no! This became evident to Woolman when he praised seven young Quaker men, conscripted to fight in George Washington's army during the Revolutionary War, when they went on a hunger strike and didn't respond to daily roll calls.

Woolman was so inspired by their example that he changed his life, stunning acquaintances when he became what today might be described as anti-American. He was, in fact, guilty of breaking the laws his countrymen held dear. Woolman wouldn't pay the war tax in 1755, remarking that it was better to "suffer patiently the distress of goods rather than pay actively."[1] But even more shocking was that Woolman quit selling gunpowder, stopped wearing dyed clothes made by the sweat of slaves, inspected the spoons he used for his meals to feel connected to the people whose hands crafted them, and chose to walk on foot rather than ride stagecoaches greased by child labor. Woolman preached regularly, but he stopped taking a fee for his ministerial services. Unlike his competitors, he never sued customers who racked up debt at his grocery store.

You don't need the nation to save you. Live a moral example. Patriotism toward a nation whose policies are hypocritical and whose citizens do thoughtless things will leave you feeling empty. Don't buy in. Being applauded as an upright citizen matters less than being a prophetic truth teller.

From Woolman's example we can see that personal choices can be revolutionary. But not all of them are. What good is purchasing local organic produce or fair-trade coffee or American-made cars if the workers who make them don't have health insurance, a living wage, or control over their workplace? Instead, fundamentally change how you understand the world and ensure that its unjust structures collapse. Remind everyone of the way that domination hidden from view shapes our sense of pleasure. How it's systemic and designed to be this way.

To get your compatriots to change what feels familiar, you have to make a scene. Discomfort is the price of freedom. That's why Woolman wouldn't write up a bill of sale for an enslaved person in 1742. He discouraged hospitality toward slaveholders and refrained from consuming products from the West Indies. He inspired gossip when he walked through town in his memorable white hat and his unbleached cotton shirts—without cuffs, ruffles, and collars, which were stylish then. Woolman didn't drink tea for reasons remarkably different than his countrymen who dumped 342 chests of it at Griffin's Wharf in Boston in 1773. The Boston Tea Party protesters thought the British Crown was tyrannical in its overreaching tea tax. Taxation without representation? This wasn't Woolman's concern. Not at all. Woolman abstained from tea because it was sweetened by unpaid slave labor.

Woolman's choices throughout his life point to a systemic analysis of power. He wasn't singling out bad investors, crooked cops, or white supremacists but rather the profit drive of capitalism, the insatiable thirst of empire, and the dehumanizing logic of racism. All are joined at the hip, entwined, mutually reinforcing, in America. "Seed sewn with the tears of a confined oppressed people, harvest cut down by an overborne discontented reaper," Woolman said, "makes bread less sweet to an honest man."[2]

When Woolman arrived in Britain in 1772 after a harrowing journey across the sea, he was uninterested in studying the intricacies of British parliamentarism or beholding the breathtaking riches of the gentry. Well aware of where the story of a nation truly lies—in the lives of ordinary people—and why it's impossible to be blindly loyal to a nation that covers up this story,

Woolman kept records of the wages paid to day laborers and female spinners; the price of butter, cheese, and
mutton; and the average cost of rent. As was customary
for him, Woolman walked through the textile regions,
where the runoff of dye leaking from wet cloth stained
his white shoes and the hellscape of horse manure and
waste overwhelmed his senses.[3] This is how you get to
know a country.

Bearing witness is a hallmark of revolutionary en-
gagement, but so is building a just world, even if it's
nowhere to be found around you. In 1763, Woolman
officiated at the wedding of a formerly enslaved Black
man, William Boen, who was part of his New Jersey
congregation. This when slavery was widespread in New
Jersey and racism was as ordinary as going to church.
Woolman organized a New Jersey association whose
goal was to purchase two thousand acres of land near
the Pine Barrens for a sovereign Indian settlement.
Woolman didn't believe that reparations for unpaid
enslaved labor was a political nonstarter—he saw it as
a moral imperative. To make something possible, you
have to give yourself permission to believe it's possible.
In the 1760s, Woolman began calculating what debt he
owed to someone who was stolen from Guinea at age

forty who worked until he died. Adding 3 percent interest and compounding it every ten years, Woolman determined that the man's children should receive about
141 pounds.[4]

Unlike the British Crown, which demanded political allegiance from him, or his Quaker community,
who wanted him to be a loyal member, Woolman never
wanted to be sanctified. He asked that his clothing be
traded away to pay for his funeral. The gravedigger who
buried him in an unmarked grave on October 9, 1772,
in York, England, worked in exchange for Woolman's
tattered white shoes. Even in death, Woolman tried to
overturn the cynicism that encourages sickening cruelty and breathtaking thoughtlessness. What a life. The
Philadelphia Quakers thought so, and in 1774, they
posthumously published 1,200 copies of Woolman's
Journal, which ran 436 pages long.

Today's activists may know nothing about this
eighteenth-century pacifist, who in his time was known
more as a curiosity than an inspiration, but you see him
among the hunger strikers across US prisons who protest living conditions that violate the UN Declaration
of Human Rights. You see him among the young kids
who walk out of school to protest the world burning,

and among the Wall of Moms who, arms locked together, form a human chain to protect from federal law
enforcement young Portland activists protesting the
police killings of unarmed Black men and women. Like
Woolman, these citizens don't ask what they can do for
their country but what their country can do for them,
and for those they've never met. To finally, perhaps for
the first time, make that country worth loving.

5

REDEFINE IDEALS TO MEET YOUR DEMOCRATIC ASPIRATIONS

National unity is seen as the solution to the divisiveness of our post-Trump era. This is what we heard from Republican leaders immediately after a deadly riot inside the Capitol building by pro-Trump white nationalists, contesting the results of the 2020 presidential election, on January 6, 2021. The stampede into the Capitol left numerous people dead and congressmembers running for cover to their offices, as a joint session was officially certifying the electoral votes to affirm Biden's presidential victory. House Democrats swiftly pressed to impeach Trump again for inciting the insurrection because he told rioters minutes before they stormed the White House: "You'll never take back our country with weakness. You have to show strength, and you have to be strong."[1] House Minority Leader Kevin McCarthy (R-CA), however, wanted reconciliation, not accountability. He wrote to his Republican caucus, "Personally, I continue to believe that an impeachment at this time would have the opposite effect of bringing our country together when we need to get America back on a path towards unity and civility."[2] McCarthy's plea implies that crises require unity, not finger-pointing. What this means is that there's some perceived magical universal "we" who can be bound together, even when the opposite is true. There's no reason to perpetuate this myth. Don't reinforce some fictional "we" that doesn't exist, but instead interrogate who "we" are. Show how prevailing stories of American identity exclude people of color. Raise troubling questions about the national narrative. Don't gloss over pandemics of violence that erase marginalized citizens or incorporate them into an American dream they never fully enjoyed. If anything, redefine who "we" are to meet your democratic aspirations.

This is what the revolutionary Pequot Indian William Apess did when, in his capacity as a Protestant preacher, he arrived in Mashpee, Massachusetts, in 1831. Mashpee was a major Indigenous town of several hundred, but it was controlled by three white overseers who held an iron grip on lucrative access to grazing rights and determined who could enter and leave town.

Even more, the overseers appointed a non-Indigenous white preacher, Rev. Phineas Fish, to the community's Old Indian Meeting House, funded and instituted by Harvard College, to preach only to white people. Not surprisingly, Fish demeaned the Mashpee and enriched himself with aid intended for them.

Immediately after Apess arrived, the Mashpee gave him a home and granted him fishing rights. They felt solidarity with his story of resistance amidst dispossession. Born on January 31, 1798, in Colrain, Massachusetts, to a shoemaker and domestic worker, Apess lived with his grandparents after his parents divorced, but he suffered from hunger, and the family couldn't afford decent clothes to keep him warm. In a formative moment when Apess was only four, his grandmother beat him. An uncle saved him, though, and petitioned to have the boy live as an indentured servant with a neighbor. It took Apess one year for what he described as his "mangled" body to recover. He was eventually sold to a Massachusetts judge and then to an aristocrat from Connecticut, before he ran away and enlisted as a drummer boy at the age of fourteen to fight in the War of 1812.

Subjugation formed the contours of Apess's early life. So, his mission became to abolish it everywhere. After arriving in Massachusetts and being taken in by the Mashpee, Apess repaid the Mashpee's kindness by collaborating with them to devise a twelve-person governing council. The council wrote a petition, the Indian Declaration of Independence, of July 1, 1833, which says: "That we, as a tribe, will rule ourselves, and have the right to do so; for all men are born free and equal, says the Constitution of the country. Resolved, That we will not permit any white man to come upon our plantation, to cut or carry off wood or hay, or any other article, without our permission, . . . That we will put said resolutions in force after that date . . . the penalty of binding and throwing them from the plantation, if they will not stay away."[3]

The Indian Declaration of Independence threatened the white ruling class when one of its national leaders, Democratic president Andrew Jackson, was busy enacting a campaign of genocide and ethnic cleansing against more than one hundred thousand Indigenous people in the 1830s across Georgia, Alabama, North Carolina, and Florida. The US Congress gave Jackson its blessing by passing the Indian Removal Act (1830). Unlike Jackson, with his strategy of violent plunder, Apess was nonviolent, though his defiant rhetoric inspired direct confrontation with power. Apess turned the US Declaration of Independence on its head. The Declaration, shameless in its racism against Indigenous people and describing them as "merciless Indian savages, whose known Rule of Warfare, is an undistinguished Destruction," is used to justify the opposite of what the framers intended: Indigenous self-determination. Apess didn't traffic in themes of brotherhood and reconciliation. He questioned whether America is a free country, while applying its universal aspiration for freedom in ways to serve his community's aspirations.

Soon, he led a group of six Mashpee men to remove timber from the wagon of a white man, who, along with an accomplice, was stealing from their land. This became known in the Boston newspapers as the Mashpee Revolt. For this, Apess was charged with rioting, fined a hefty sum, and jailed for thirty days. But Apess caught the attention of the Boston antislavery abolitionist William Lloyd Garrison after the Mashpee addressed a special session of the Massachusetts state legislature on January 21, 1834. Three days later, Garrison wrote an editorial in his newspaper, *The Liberator*, reprinting parts of the Indian Declaration of Independence and condemning how whites held the Mashpee in the "chains of a servile dependence."[4]

Apess's example lived on after him in the feminist suffragist Elizabeth Cady Stanton's "Declaration of Sentiments," which, in 1848, asserted before a crowd of three hundred in Seneca Falls, New York, that "all men and women are created equal" and that "the history of mankind is a history of repeated injuries and usurpations on the part of man toward woman, having in direct object the establishment of an absolute tyranny over her."[5] Or recall the Black abolitionist Frederick Douglass's speech in Corinthian Hall in Rochester, New York, "What to a Slave Is the Fourth of July?," four years after Stanton's, in 1852. Not long after the US Congress passed the Fugitive Slave Act of 1850, which granted slave catchers the power to capture formerly enslaved fugitives in the North and return them to bondage, Douglass reminded his country, "The rich inheritance of justice, liberty, prosperity and independence, bequeathed by your fathers, is shared by you, not by me."[6]

Imagine if this approach is what our leaders had taken up on the Senate and House floors, as they returned to their chambers to certify Joe Biden's presidential victory hours after the insurrection at the Capitol? What if they had highlighted the insidious connection between whiteness and America, which made the predominately white rioters feel entitled to storm the citadel of American democracy? As if any violence they enacted was justified simply because the nation belonged to them, and to them alone? What if our leaders had said that Trump was a symptom of a legacy of a decadent empire, and that it was time not simply for an impeachment—as if excising one person from public consciousness is the only thing we need—but for a re-founding? What if they had used the Declaration of Independence's democratic ideals to argue for a living wage and Medicare for All? What if rather than fortifying the US Capitol with a metal fence—which is what they did—they demanded that representative democracy, composed of institutions like the filibuster, the Electoral College, and federalism, all of which are steeped in racist origins, be broken down and started anew? If you ask these questions after the next crisis, you can help ensure that January 6 never happens again.

6

POLITICIZE TRUTH

Truth is in crisis. Look at the cover stories in *Time* titled "How Your Brain Tricks You into Believing Fake News," and *The Atlantic*, "How America Lost Its Mind."[1] Journalists lament the rise of disinformation. They worry the end of democracy is near. Can you blame them?

For four years, the Trump administration lied with reckless abandon. About things major—banning travelers from predominately Muslim countries in 2017, it said, was about national security, not Islamophobia. And things minor—the crowd at Trump's inauguration, said White House press secretary Sean Spicer, was the largest in history. The lying has continued even since Trump has left office. The right-wing cable-news ecosystem of *Fox News* provides its devotees with what Trump senior advisor Kellyanne Conway once called "alternative facts." "Climate skeptics" say global warming is a hoax. Armchair epidemiologists object to data that COVID-19 is really that lethal. Anti-vaxxers pose as health experts to say that routine vaccinations for seasonal influenza are dangerous.

How to confront this? One common solution we hear is that we need to recommit ourselves to truth. You know the list: Rigor in research. Impartiality. Greater transparency. Follow the facts, even if you don't like them. If it were only that simple. Yes, truth is indispensable for creating a shared community of trust, but in politics, what matters isn't simply that you tell the truth but rather how you shape the context, dramatic narratives, and stakes of the facts involved. There are many ways to tell a story. When you tell the truth, highlight the hidden forces of power that determine who gets what and who gets nothing. Foreground that what we believe is a product of struggle. Highlight who gets to speak, whose voices are heard, and what questions are worth asking. Find historical precedents. We've been here before. The past haunts the present. Don't sugarcoat what's bitter.

This is how freedom fighters battled the greatest disinformation campaign in US history. Not in 2021 but after the US Civil War. By the 1870s, southern states including Georgia, Alabama, North Carolina, and Mississippi were hell-bent on rolling back the gains for newly enfranchised Black men during Reconstruction (1865–1877). This after the Thirteenth Amendment to the US Constitution abolished slavery, the Fourteenth provided equal protection under the law, and the Fifteenth guaranteed the right to vote to men of color.

Southerners may have invented fake news with what they called the "Lost Cause," which omitted slavery as the catalyst for the Civil War. In best-selling books written by Joel Chandler Harris and Thomas Nelson Page, and through monuments to Confederate leaders Robert E. Lee and Jefferson Davis, the war was described by southern redeemers as being about states' rights. This re-education campaign served white supremacy incredibly well. For if, as they said, southerners only cared about preserving their own culture and were uninterested in dominating Black citizens, then, surely, the 1890s Jim Crow era was harmless. According to this view, the trauma of the poll tax, the grandfather clause, residential segregation, the chain gang, sharecropping, and the epidemic of lynching was no big deal.

No one confronted historical whitewashing as courageously as the most famous Black abolitionist in history, Frederick Douglass. It's not enough to tell the truth, Douglass believed. If you're invested in liberation, you need to identify friends and enemies, what you will and won't stand for and against. Standing in front of the Tomb of the Civil War Unknowns in Arlington National Cemetery on Memorial Day to commemorate the end of the Civil War in 1871, Douglass said, let's not forget the "difference between the parties," those who "struck at the nation's life and those who struck to save it—those who fought for slavery and those who fought for liberty and justice."[2]

Memory is a battlefield. Drawing attention to political fault lines makes you know reconciliation isn't easily achievable, that racial justice won't be quickly achieved. "It was a war of ideas, a battle of principles," Douglass says in 1878.[3] Concrete ideology, not human folly, was at the heart of the Civil War. There's no equivalence between the Black and white experience. There are victims and perpetrators. Innocent bystanders are few and far between. Keep in mind the different experiences of the same event. If slavery is a bountiful festival for slaveholders, then it's a festival of violence for the enslaved. Douglass says it is "traced like that of a wounded man through a crowd by the blood."[4] The past is never fully vanquished. History doesn't move in a linear progressive direction, toward ever greater justice; it zig zags and ebbs and flows, cycling from despair to hope, terror to liberation, and back again. "The South has a past not to be contemplated with pleasure, but with a shudder," Douglass declares. "She has been selling agony, trading in blood and in the souls of men. If her past has any lesson, it is one of repentance and through reformation."[5]

You'll soon hear former Trump administration officials wanting to be rehabilitated in the public sphere, cashing in on lucrative speaking gigs and book contracts. They'll say they were just following orders when they designed policies to put brown children seeking asylum in cages on the US-Mexico border. Or, they'll say, they were involved in a vigorous behind-the-scenes pushback you just didn't see. It's not that hard to imagine Trump, at some future dinner with his presidential predecessors—Bill Clinton, George W. Bush, and Barack Obama—being toasted as a political disruptor who "shook up" Washington, inspired disaffected voters to get involved, and was smart for getting tough on China.

With the memory of Trump's administration still fresh in your mind, follow Douglass's example. Never forget the cheating, lying, corruption, racism, faux populism, sexism, homophobia, warmongering, assault on environmental protections, privatization, tax cuts for the rich, the Muslim ban, and the packing of the courts with far-right judges. But go beyond remembering Trump's presidency. Next time you see college students toppling Confederate statues in Virginia or North Carolina, know that they are dismantling white supremacy in our cherished public spaces. In doing this, they aren't promoting a "cancel" culture that signals the end of free speech. They're forming a counterweight to reactionary politics. How else to counter Trump's threat to defund public schools that teach the *New York Times*'s 1619 Project—an award-winning series of essays investigating slavery in the US—and to veto a defense bill that renamed military bases still carrying the names of vanquished Confederate generals? Never forget that truth is a story. The stories we tell about past disasters ensure they don't happen again.

7

IMAGINE UTOPIA

When the world is crumbling beneath our feet, we're told we need a strong dose of common sense. Do what's sensible rather than what's ideal. This was Barack Obama's message when he bailed out banks deemed "too big to fail" after they unleashed the Great Recession of 2008. It was sensible, he argued, to bail out the banks that had orchestrated the subprime mortgage debacle that wiped out a large chunk of US middle-class wealth. Think, more recently, about when the US Congress gave a trillion dollars in grants and tax breaks to major corporations after the COVID pandemic in 2020 left millions unemployed.

Here's the secret about practicality: it pays rich dividends for the powerful. Just look at the profits that corporations turned during the pandemic—Facebook ($84 billion in revenue in 2020, compared to $70 billion in 2019), Amazon ($386 billion in revenue compared to

$280 billion), Walmart ($520 billion in net global sales, compared to $510 billion). Practicality is the last thing you want when our world is in flux. Disaster is the best time to expand your imagination. When the cracks expose the façade of normalcy, an alternative future can be glimpsed. Embrace the impossible. Imagine utopia. It's a future where needless suffering is gone. Where creativity is encouraged. A world in which people work and live, not live to work. Don't be afraid of idealism!

This has been done before. It can be done again. Almost two centuries ago, Americans turned to the utopian imagination because the early fires of the Industrial Revolution were raging uncontrollably. If you were able to look beyond the smog-polluted air and past the gut-wrenching poverty, you'd see mind-numbing and backbreaking work in factories. Children, as young as five, were exploited in obscene ways, making up approximately 40 percent of the mill employees in New England in the 1820s. Young women recruited from rural Massachusetts would feverishly work eighty-hour workweeks in the cotton textile factories in Waltham, for the famed industrialist Francis Cabot Lowell's Boston Manufacturing Company. The crisis of work at the dawn of capitalism broke more spirits than we can count.

So, if you were there, what would you have heard from the industrialists and their apologists looking to keep their operations flowing seamlessly? Perhaps they would have conceded that it's unfortunate, yes, but "there's nothing we can about it! It's natural." History has arrived. Sure, you can accept these arguments. Or you can do something else: choose life over death, and do everything you can to tell the world why.

On the day that Thomas Jefferson died, July 4, 1826—the fiftieth anniversary of the Declaration of Independence—Robert Owen, a former manager of the New Lanark cotton mills in Scotland, did just that. He gave a rousing speech in New Harmony, Indiana, a small rural town of several hundred. At the time, Owen was two years into presiding over what became one of the most well-known, even if short-lived, American utopian communal experiments. Within weeks of arriving in the US, the charming and soft-spoken Owen, rather than spread the gospel of industriousness, made elites listen to his criticisms. Individualism is soulless. Marriage is coercive. Organized religion impoverishes the soul.

Remember: radical ideas are most palatable when they're boldly announced and proudly defended in the mainstream. Go to the halls of power and tell the ruling class why they're wrong! Owen spoke with presidential candidate and soon-to-be president John Quincy Adams, and he visited Thomas Jefferson's and James Madison's homes, and even gave two speeches before Congress on Capitol Hill. He sent copies of his pamphlets to Napoleon Bonaparte and had a model replica print of his ideal town proudly displayed in President Quincy Adams's White House. What is practical is what we agree can be done, should be done. Nothing wrought by people occurs naturally. "The members of any community may by degrees be trained to live without idleness, without poverty, without crime, and without punishment," Owen said, "for each of these is the effect of error in the various systems prevalent throughout the world. . . . Train any population rationally, and they will be rational."[1]

To build a new world, you need to imagine what it might look like. Otherwise, you can't move beyond what's familiar. Meticulously design your utopia, even if you're chastised as naïve. In the blueprint for Owen's New Harmony, kitchens, gardens, libraries, and stores were surrounded by factories and farmlands. Work wasn't the center of life, and leisure wasn't a frivolous luxury. It was essential. Though the blueprint wasn't built with the 240,000 bricks Owen himself purchased, what emerged in the commune of New Harmony was stunning regardless. If you walked through the village, you'd see economic equality between the eight hundred to nine hundred farmers and mechanics who took up residence there. Class distinctions and hierarchies between professions collapsed because residents held that all work ought to be dignified, and that no one was exceptional, above the rest. A "Constitution of the Community of Equality" was ratified by the entire community, enshrining the "equality of rights, uninfluenced by sex or condition," and "equality of duties."[2] The constitution guaranteed every adult twenty-one and older an equal vote and gave them a right to the land, as well as everything produced upon it. Every Tuesday there was a neighborhood dance led by a brass orchestra, and people addressed each other by their first names, a move that would have scandalized many accustomed to the mores of polite society. Working mothers—for a small fee—could send their children to a communal daycare, where the youngsters learned through playing games rather than memorizing equations.

The beautiful thing about utopian experiments is that because they shock the senses and inspire dreams to begin anew—no matter how flawed or incomplete they might be—they live on as a testament for future generations. That's what happened a thousand miles northeast of New Harmony fifteen years later. Brook Farm was founded in 1841 by Unitarian minister George Ripley and his partner, Sophia, on pastureland and wild forests in West Roxbury, Massachusetts, at the time nine miles outside of Boston proper. Like New Harmony, the Brook Farm commune was populated by feminists, abolitionists, writers, and fine artists. It operated as a joint-stock company, which meant that profits from agricultural work were shared. And Brook Farm residents edited a literary review, *The Dial*.

The towering essayist Ralph Waldo Emerson never joined Brook Farm, but he frequently visited, preaching what was its gospel and should be ours: Self-reliance is about cultivating moral character. Democracy will be eroded through the pursuit of private property. "Reliance on Property," Emerson concluded in 1844, "including the reliance on governments which protect it, is the want of self-reliance. . . . Whilst the rights of all persons are equal . . . their rights in property are very unequal. One man owns his clothes, and another owns a country. . . . Property demands a government framed on the ratio of owners and of owning."[3]

As part of a collectivist "phalanx," inspired by the increasingly popular "associationist" ideas of the French socialist Charles Fourier—around 15,000 Americans were involved with Fourierist movements in the nineteenth century—Brook Farm is an example of how to make democracy work for social cooperation, and vice versa. It had a school for children that blurred the line between art and work. Geography, poetry, dancing, literature, and music were taught while children were out working the fields, for which they were paid ten cents a day. On weekends, there were lectures on the philosophy of Baruch Spinoza and vigorous discussions about the economic value of collectivism. The initial makeup of Brook Farm was New England elites like the Ripleys. But this didn't hold for long, and it soon gave way to something more inclusive. Shoemakers, carpenters, and other artisans joined, because they were drawn to the hope of freedom.

The freedom dreams behind nineteenth-century utopian experiments live on in unexpected ways. Utopia can't be fully policed or restricted to the few, no matter how hard they might try. It belongs to those who claim it as their own. Consider that Black women, who were written out of New Harmony's exclusionary racial covenant, and were nowhere to be found on Brook Farm, established in 2020 the Freedom Georgia Initiative on ninety-six acres of rural land in Toomsboro. Envisioned as a Black-centric community, the initiative aims to address legacies of racial domination. Its long-term goal? Providing economic and cultural development. Freedom Georgia was born exactly when a new world was necessary: the year that Ahmaud Arbery, Tony McDade, George Floyd, and Breonna Taylor were murdered and the COVID-19 pandemic devastated Black families. College students in small towns and big cities spontaneously design collective living spaces, where they share meals, housework, music, and friendship. Bookshelves of revolutionary literature, science fiction, and the occult form the backdrop for young people who envision liberation in the realms of work, race, gender, and sexuality. Utopia isn't something you should abandon just to prove your maturity. Utopia reignites hope for growing up and growing old. Have faith that growing up is a worthwhile activity to be embraced, not a mindless chore to be tolerated.

8

QUESTION ELITES

The elite maintain their power depending on how they exhibit leadership in crisis. They know this, especially since a long-standing political belief is that in troubled times, we need good stewardship—a steady hand navigating a ship through the eye of the storm to get us ashore. During the Trump years, the "chaos" of the White House is what left so many journalists disturbed. Incoherent and disorganized, deranged and unhinged, was how they described his style. But be careful what you wish for. Imagine if Trump had displayed muscular leadership during his four years in office. We would have been at war with China and Russia, witnessed the censoring of free speech in leading newspapers, and seen the crushing of the Black Lives Matter protests with the full force of the US army. Elite leadership after disaster can be an existential threat for democracy. By no means is it a precondition for a well-functioning society. So, question leaders who claim to know best. Expose how they neglect, if not intensify, the precariousness of the most vulnerable. You don't need a PhD from Harvard to know that war benefits weapon manufacturers, not soldiers and civilians, who are its collateral damage. You don't need to be an economist to know that middle-class wealth is nothing compared to that of the super-rich. People can rule themselves. Be free. Be spontaneous.

No one devoted her life to raising awareness about the danger of elite rule as much as the anarchist Emma Goldman. Before she became known as "Red Emma" and world famous for her impassioned speeches to thousands by assailing the monstrosity of Gilded Age capitalism in relation to the tenement houses in New York's Lower East Side in the 1890s, Goldman was a refugee from arbitrary power. She arrived in the US with her sister to escape an arranged marriage and her abusive father, Abraham, who blamed her for a sexual assault she experienced as a teen in a hotel in St. Petersburg, where she and her Orthodox Jewish family lived. Goldman resolved to never return to tsarist Russia or to the Jewish village in Kovno, Lithuania, where she was born on June 27, 1869.

Revolutionaries aren't products of a divine miracle. They're made. A spark inflames your sense of purpose, shining a bright light upon what was dark before. You're moved to act. One night, after working a grueling ten-hour day at a job for which she earned fifty cents a week, in Rochester, New York, a seventeen-year-old Goldman read about the event that would change everything for her: the Haymarket Massacre in Chicago. On May 4, 1886, a rally was held in Haymarket Square to support the general strike being held for an eight-hour workday. The rally in Haymarket was one of 1,400 held throughout the country over the next few weeks and included, in total, almost half a million participants. At the Haymarket rally, a bomb exploded. Seven policemen and eleven demonstrators died. Eight Chicago labor leaders, proud anarchists, were charged, even though they hadn't thrown the explosive. Four of them were hanged a year later, in 1887. When she heard a woman enthusiastically endorse their execution, saying that's just what the murderers deserved, Goldman leapt at her throat, screaming, "I will kill you!"[1]

Why was Goldman enraged? Because the American government was doing what it always does when the public is stunned—asserting its power to secure its crumbling authority. At the time, singling out anarchists was an effective way to scare the ascendent labor movement, which was being driven by the waves of immigrants arriving from Eastern Europe. Goldman wouldn't stand for it. So, she made Haymarket into a symbol for what became Goldman's lifelong enemy: Unchecked authority, ruthless in its hypocrisy and shameless in its conduct. Power that creates the disorder it then claims to resolve. "Organized authority [gives] greater privileges to those who have already monopolized the earth . . . further enslaving the disinherited masses," she declared. "Government—laws, police, soldiers, the courts, legislatures, prisons—is strenuously engaged in 'harmonizing' the most antagonistic elements in society."[2]

Words matter. Damning, inflamed, intense, agitated turns of phrase—rippling with a frenzied cadence—make you reassess what it means to be a citizen. It's not violence, but vivid arguments that speak to your life, that make you believe transformation is possible. Violence doesn't work. Because when violence erupts, the public gets outraged and the government is more repressive. Recall that the assassination of President William McKinley by an overzealous anarchist in 1901 led to the congressional passage of the repressive Alien Immigration Act of 1903, which banned and expelled anarchists. Or the failed killing of union-busting industrialist Henry Clay Frick by Alexander Berkman, Goldman's longtime confidant, on July 23, 1892, which led not to revolutionary change but to Berkman being jailed for fourteen years.

The great lesson of anarchism is that revolutionary writing is more dangerous than one-off sensational deeds. Arguments are contagious. Remember that Goldman's pride and joy was her journal, *Mother Earth*, which she founded in 1906 and remained in print until 1917. When her book *Anarchism and Other Essays* was published in 1910, she traveled to 37 cities and gave 120 lectures. Write a pamphlet demanding emancipation! Or a protest ballad that turns conventional social norms on their head!

Arguments are vital for movement building. Elites know this well. In 1919, as Goldman was being released from a two-year federal prison sentence in Missouri for printing a hundred thousand copies of a manifesto she wrote encouraging US soldiers to dodge the First World War, for which she was later to be deported to the Soviet Union, the man who would eventually become the FBI director, J. Edgar Hoover, called her the "most dangerous women in America." No wonder. Hoover knew that when you open your eyes to the way the state is a coercive force and to the realization that crime, as Goldman said, isn't a product of natural deviant behavior but of social ills that can be fixed, "naught but misdirected energy,"[3] you think differently. No longer do you bow down before the national security apparatus. You no longer tell everyone, in a compulsory rite of passage, that you support the troops. You instead focus on creating institutions of social support that give people resources to rule themselves.

Much of how we think about who should rule depends on the image of what we think they would do. But no one knows what people would do in a world that looks nothing like ours. In 1897, a labor leader asked Goldman what her vision for a free society was. Her response: "I am really too much of an anarchist to work out a program for the members of that society; in fact, I do not bother about such trifling details; all I want is freedom, perfect, unrestricted liberty for myself and others."[4] You'll never know the future, but you could say that if liberation is to be realized in the future, who you are and what you do must be fluid. Consider that Goldman worked as a nurse midwife by day and organized with the Amalgamated Workers Union by night. She supported birth control and free love, which put her at odds with some puritanical suffragists who celebrated marriage. She was inspired by the Bolshevik Revolution of 1917 but later became disillusioned and ended her stay in the Soviet Union soon after the Kronstadt rebellion.

She couldn't stomach watching striking sailors, agitating for better food rations, representative elections, and free speech, being crushed by Leon Trotsky and his Red Army in March 1921.

·········

Be open to new possibilities. A widely discussed story that cemented Goldman's status as a folk hero is that when she was scolded for dancing—for being too carefree, uninhibited, in charge of her own movements—during a serious anarchist organizing meeting, she responded, that if she couldn't dance, she wouldn't come to your revolution.[5] Dancing is an apt metaphor for how to understand freedom. Freedom, like dance, breathes and moves, changing to the rhythm of those who are there—who move their bodies and feel the world.

Move spontaneously. Be poetic. Let loose. Collaborate. Question elites. Who needs cops when you are free from starvation? Create massive investments in art and culture. Why not cancel billionaires? Destroy nuclear weapons? Once everyday people no longer appear as a bloodthirsty mob, you relax your need for control and can dream alongside them. How beautiful.

The harrowing explosion that rocked Haymarket Square reverberated for years in Goldman's heart, long after the rubble was cleared in 1886 and up until she died of a stroke at the age of seventy in 1940 in Toronto. Goldman asked to be buried in Forest Park, Illinois, next to the Haymarket Martyrs Monument, where pilgrims to this day visit her grave with flowers and recite poems to commemorate her legacy. But if you ask our leaders, anarchism, like Goldman's memory, is still a grave menace to society. How else to explain the decision of Trump's attorney general William Barr in September 2020 to label New York, Portland, and Seattle "anarchist jurisdictions"—and, thus, seek to withhold federal funds from those cities? This, in response to the Black Lives Matter protests that gripped the nation with the call to defund the police. The demonized anarchist of Barr's nightmares, like J. Edgar Hoover's, is dressed in black from head to toe, hides their face behind a mask, and holds a Molotov cocktail while spewing foul language, itching to break windows and instill mayhem at midnight. This is a caricature. But it's good for distracting attention from the way anarchism is at the forefront of community-revitalization work, without which democracy wouldn't be the same.

What is anarchism today? It's found in prison-abolition groups like Critical Resistance in Oakland, New York, and Philly, working to end US mass incarceration. In the Food Not Bombs program. Community-run bookstores and book publishers like AK Press. Social workers distributing hot meals for the unsheltered. Vegans spearheading the animal rights movement. If the ruling class attended any of these gatherings, they might bristle at the irreverence, shudder at the passion, and wilt in the face of righteous indignation. They might declare a riot. Or scold attendees to get jobs. But there's no need to think like elites. Or echo their fearmongering. That's not your job. It's theirs. It's best if you, like Goldman, dance like no one's watching, with reckless abandon, to the beat of freedom, even as the flames of disaster are encircling you. Others will be inspired to do the same and join your revolution. This might allow the fire of law-and-order politics to be extinguished once and for all.

9

MAKE PEACE

National security is one of the few areas Democrats and Republicans agree upon. Intelligence agencies like the CIA, NSA, and FBI are revered, and the US military is the most respected public institution across political lines. The Pentagon's yearly budget is over one trillion dollars. There are eight hundred US military bases across the world. When Democrats and Republicans talk about foreign policy, they mean maintaining US superpower status globally. If this is the case in times of peace, in times of conflict, deference to the national security apparatus intensifies. Consider that when it became widely reported that Russia meddled during the 2016 presidential election to support Donald Trump's candidacy, there was a swift condemnation from both sides. Calls for serious retaliation eventually translated into economic sanctions upon Russian oligarchs. A decade before, in 2003, Republican president George W.

Bush made the dubious claim, entirely manufactured by his intelligence agencies, that Saddam Hussein's Iraq had stockpiled weapons of mass destruction. Vaunted publications like the *New York Times* ran stories affirming it. Before long, America was at war. Again.

But war isn't the answer. Fight for peace. Do it immediately when hawks set the stage for violent foreign excursions. With urgency. Don't wait until the war begins.

This was the message of the first mass antiwar movement in the US. As World War I exploded in Europe, shortly after Archduke Ferdinand of Austria was assassinated in Sarajevo on June 28, 1914, by a nineteen-year-old Bosnian Serb nationalist, Gavrilo Princip, the US, led by President Woodrow Wilson, proclaimed a position of neutrality in "thought and deed." Wilson's decision to stay out of the conflict was broadly supported by the American public, whose many nationalities—German, Hungarian, French, Russian, English—represented the nations in battle across the Atlantic. But the temptation to exert US superpower status, as well as the massive economic opportunities of a war economy, proved too great for Wilson and his allies. By 1915, war hawks were pushing for what became known as the "preparedness" movement, which involved the buildup of land and naval forces—a move endorsed by former president Theodore Roosevelt. This was the man who made his political chops as an advocate of US empire during the Spanish-American War of 1898. J. P. Morgan and Company didn't need to be persuaded to join the war effort; it was already financing the Allies in Europe.[1]

So, the wheels had been long set in motion when Wilson issued a toothless ultimatum in 1917 that the US would violate its neutrality if German U-boats attacked American sailors. Given the German kaiser's reliance on submarine warfare, Wilson couldn't have been surprised when the line was crossed in March of that year after three US merchant vessels were sunk. A month later, on April 2, Wilson got the approval he wanted from Congress. The nation was at war.

There's a moral to this story. War must be opposed long before it appears as an imminent threat. By the time the first bombs drop, and the troops hit the ground on foreign territory, flags are raised and critical thinking is abandoned. You are presented with the false choice of glorious victory or shameful defeat. Remember: any successful peace movement must match the aggressiveness of war making. Build an army of the willing unwilling to compromise peace.

One of the first mass antiwar demonstrations was held in New York, where, at the end of a cloudy day in August 1914, 1,500 women who had been involved in the decades-long struggle for women's suffrage marched down Fifth Avenue dressed entirely in either black or white.[2] By January 1915, a conference of suffragists had organized the Woman's Peace Party in Washington, DC. A year later, the party had expanded to forty thousand members and two hundred branches nationwide. Its newly elected president, Jane Addams, who met with Woodrow Wilson frequently, was no stranger to progressive politics in her ferocious support of public education and economic equality.

Addams had become well-known through her book *Newer Ideals of Peace* (1907), in which she advocated a social philosophy of nurture over antagonism, and for her founding of Hull House, which she opened in 1889 for working-class Chicagoans on the city's industrial, immigrant West Side. "Was not war in the interest of democracy for the salvation of civilization a contradiction of terms," Addams asked, "whoever said it or however often it was repeated?"[3] Rallies, demonstrations, newspaper ads, and lobbying efforts would consume the peace movement for the next year. Their hard work was made visible one month into the war, in May 1917. The

People's Council of America for Democracy and Peace held its inaugural event at Madison Square Garden, which twenty thousand New Yorkers attended.

Some of those who showed up were official delegates of the American Union Against Militarism. Its leader at the time was the Harvard-educated civil libertarian and St. Louis social worker Roger Baldwin. Baldwin called himself an "unhappy optimist," because he did everything in his power to end the tyrannical reign of the hawks. "I cannot consistently . . . violate an act which seems to me to be a denial of everything which ideally and in practice I hold sacred," Baldwin said, providing the intellectual foundation for conscientious objectors, who were swelling in ranks by the end of the decade.[4] Three million men didn't register for the draft. And at least 350,000 registered but didn't show up for their basic training or medical examinations, and, even more, wouldn't accept alternative work like farming. They deserted. But they were lucky. They lived. By the time the armistice was declared and the fighting stopped, in November 1918, a hundred thousand Americans had perished, and millions more were seriously wounded.[5]

A war mentality means you'll prosecute anyone who violates your ideals. But a peace mindset means to relinquish thinking in terms of "us vs. them." Peace means honoring the dignity of all, regardless of how they make you feel or what they've done. No one deserves to be bombed and maimed.

Roger Baldwin knew he had to match the fervor of President Wilson—worried about the unabating tide of dissent in the country—who was a shadow of the reluctant pacifist he ran as during his reelection campaign in 1916. By 1917, Wilson was an aggressive nationalist, emboldened by the June passage of the Espionage Act, which gave his government authority to censor the content of newspapers, to deport hundreds of so-called traitors who handed out antiwar pamphlets, and to threaten draft dodgers with twenty years in prison and a ten-thousand-dollar fine. Baldwin and the National Civil Liberties Bureau (which would become known as the American Civil Liberties Union in 1920) couldn't wage their crusade in the courts, which were hostile toward the right of dissent. This became exceedingly clear in 1919, when the US Supreme Court unanimously decided, in *Schenck v. United States*, to uphold the government's right to jail Charles Schenck, a socialist who had distributed fifteen thousand antiwar pamphlets, for six months. In such a climate, Baldwin had to go before the court of public opinion by sponsoring prominent liberal intellectuals on speaking tours, organizing letter-writing campaigns, and lobbying elected officials.

Peace advocates are always in a race against the clock. Even if this current administration doesn't send troops abroad, it's only a matter of time before another does. Contemporary weapons manufacturers like Lockheed Martin, Northrop Grumman, and Raytheon, on whose executive board Biden's defense secretary, Lloyd Austin, sat and in which he held $1.4 million in stock options, have combined for yearly revenues of almost $100 billion. There's an army of lobbyists in DC whose job is to convince congressmembers that a robust national security position wins elections. We're always on the brink of disaster. War is easy. Peace is hard. To win a war, you need weapons to annihilate everything in sight, to bring your enemy to their knees. To win peace, you need to create conditions that end conflict: Destroy poverty. Guarantee universal education. Support direct democracy. This can't be calculated by the number of buildings bombed or enemy soldiers killed. But it's our best hope.

10

BUILD A DEMOCRATIC SOCIETY

Faith in democratic institutions was obliterated during the Trump era. Honestly, even before that, it had been on life support for decades: Congressional gridlock. The corporate media's profit-based coverage model that focuses on the most sensational of stories. Courts, increasingly dominated by right-wing judges, that are unresponsive to popular demands. That was bad enough. Then, Trump turned the presidency into a slot machine to enrich himself and his family. No wonder Americans are desperate for stability. "Everybody wants a return to some kind of normalcy, but given all the stuff that Trump got away with, people are wondering if that's possible," said a senior fellow at the Brookings Institution in Washington, DC.[1]

For many Americans, restoring our democratic values means guaranteeing checks and balances between branches of government. It means respecting our political opponents and learning from competing perspectives. Pundits pine for courageous politicians and nonpartisan public servants who keep the wheels of good government humming along. But a crisis in democracy is when you should broaden what democracy means. That's when you say democracy isn't about responsible political leadership but, rather, say it is about socioeconomic equality and the collaborative practices of collective rule. It's not enough to vote or join a political campaign every election cycle. Revolutionize your life so that corrosive forms of hierarchy are withered away. Grassroots organization and direct action, based in how you want society to be reorganized, is a fountain of energy that replenishes your sense of purpose and reminds you what you care about. When disaster strikes, make a community based in unconditional hospitality. Forge local networks.

The 1930s are reminiscent of today. That's when democracy was under siege in the US. Fascism and nativism were on the rise, promising national redemption through isolationism and racist cultural restoration. The key figures were the Nazi-sympathizing American aviator, Charles Lindbergh, and the Catholic preacher from Michigan, Charles Coughlin, whose weekly antisemitic broadcasts reached millions. The US Communist

Party, on the other hand, thought democracy could be achieved through international class consciousness. This made sense, especially when unemployment hit 30 percent. Dorothy Day disagreed with both approaches. She despised racists, and though an advocate for the workers' movement, she distrusted political parties. Democracy, she believed, is a grassroots activity for everyone.

Born in Brooklyn, New York, in 1897 to a lower-middle-class Protestant family, Day became a carefree atheist when she enrolled at the University of Illinois, where she studied to become a journalist. But something changed for her after she was jailed for picketing Woodrow Wilson's White House in 1917 for women's suffrage, and then joined a hunger strike while imprisoned. The feeling that you can pressure the system with very little stuck with Day. She experienced it again after meeting an itinerant French peasant and street philosopher, Peter Maurin, twenty years her senior, in December 1932. Maurin changed Day's life through preaching "personalism," which he did by living in a state of voluntary poverty in a communal environment on ten acres, "Mary Farm," in rural Pennsylvania. He visited condemned prisoners and broke bread with the homeless in New York's Bowery district. "He made you feel that you and all men had great and generous hearts with which to love God," Day recalled. "If you once recognized this fact in yourself you would expect and find it in others."[2]

Day spread this gospel. A year later, at the end of a May Day celebration organized by communists, she distributed the first issues of the *Catholic Worker*, which started the movement of the same name. But reforms that made improvements around the edges weren't enough. Day wanted to revolutionize life for those who are considered disposable. Within two years, the *Catholic Worker* had amassed 150,000 readers and became the springboard for Houses of Hospitality, which provided food, shelter, clothing, prayer, and money to the poor and unsheltered across the country. That's where Day began to live—a far cry from her time in the 1920s socializing with artists and bohemians in New York's Greenwich Village, where the playwright Eugene O'Neill was among her best friends. A life in struggle is more significant than how you're socially perceived, she believed. A friend once described taking Day, then in her sixties, in tattered clothes to shop at a local secondhand store. Day didn't care if clothing was stylish. She only bought things that were ethically made.

Ethics. This is why Day and the *Catholic Worker* advocated direct action. Even as reformists in the 1930s were pining for the importance of free and fair elections as an antidote to rising global authoritarianism, Day famously looked askance at the ballot box. She didn't believe in petitioning elected officials or engaging in letter-writing campaigns. Why? Both were too far removed from real change.

Rather than read newspapers to keep up with what's happening in the world, go see it yourself. Then you'll know how policy impacts people's lives. You'll also realize that only through collective activity will you crush what Day called the "filthy, rotten system."[3] In 1936, New York sailors went on strike to oppose their ineffective union, the AFL, and the profit-seeking shipowners who wanted them to work long days for little pay. So, Day rented a vacant warehouse a block away from the waterfront and spent $4,000 feeding the strikers. The same year, Day heard of the Flint sit-down in Michigan, called the "strike of the century" because it lasted several months and featured 140,000 GM workers. She climbed through a window to join them. In 1937, Day went to interview workers at the Chicago Republic Steel Plant, who were shot by police. This was her message to workers: "Join your union and see that it is a workers' union and not a company union. Work for it."[4]

The price of Day's outspokenness was arrest. This happened in the 1950s, when she staged sit-ins demonstrating against New York's annual nuclear war simulations, and in the 1960s, when she was among the first to publicly burn draft cards during the Vietnam War. At one antiwar event held at New York's Union Square in 1965, before a crowd of several thousand, she declared, "We are the rich. The works of mercy are the opposite of the works of war, feeding the hungry, sheltering the homeless, nursing the sick, visiting the prisoner."[5] Day's last arrest came on the picket line in 1973, several years before she died. There, she stood with Cesar Chavez and his striking United Farm Workers' Union in the lettuce fields and vineyards demanding that growers renew workers' contracts.

Democracy is being in solidarity with members of your community. It's the Amazon workers in Besse-mer, Alabama, trying to unionize their workforce at a shipping center, where they have ten-hour shifts, few bathroom breaks, and walk miles every day. This work is barely tolerable for machines. But to add insult to in-jury, they have been deemed essential workers during the COVID-19 pandemic. This makes them more likely to get infected and is what helps Amazon's yearly earn-ings exceed forecasters' wildest expectations.

Democracy is also Southerners on New Ground (SONG), an LGBTQ advocacy group focusing on ra-

cial and economic justice in the south. SONG part-
nered with immigration activists in July 2014, when
they staged a sit-in front of Rep. Mark Takano's (D-CA)
Capitol Hill office to pressure the Obama administration to cease deporting migrants and to recognize the
unique precariousness of undocumented LGBTQ people. Day would have been proud.

But you can do it yourself. Build a democratic in-
frastructure when existing institutions collapse. Don't
wait for the next election. Do it whenever and wherever
you can.

ORGANIZE

Disaster accelerates the speed of decision-making. Emergency collapses time—making the past irrelevant and the future uncertain. What remains is a politics of quick fixes. When this happens, it's hard to fight against oppression. Hastily reacting to every crisis will never revolutionize society. At best, it will temporarily lessen society's inequities. What you need instead is strategy. Thoughtful organization and concrete demands that anchor you, forcing leaders to respond to your desires. Not theirs. Beware: elites will divide you from those with whom you share interests. They will intimidate you or hold out lucrative incentives for you to cave. Hold firm. You have numbers, and without your participation they can't win. Once you organize, success is within reach.

This is the great lesson of the US labor movement, even though the odds were stacked against it. At the end

of the nineteenth century, rank-and-file union membership expanded from one hundred thousand to almost
one million, and between 1880 and 1905, seven and a half
million workers took part in over thirty-eight thousand
strikes. Big business wasn't pleased. So, from the early
1900s through the 1930s, in what became infamously
known as the Lochner Era, it was enthralled to watch
the US Supreme Court provide them relief. In a series
of devastating decisions, the high court gutted popular legislation that secured workers' rights. In *Lochner
v. New York* (1905), for example, a 5–4 majority struck
down a New York state law limiting bakers' workday to
ten hours. This was the precedent for judicial activist
decisions like *Adair v. United States* (1908), which inval-
idated a congressional act that banned employers from
firing railroad workers who joined unions, and *Adkins
v. Children's Hospital* (1923), which overturned federal
minimum wage legislation for children and women. For
decades, the court held that freedom of contract and
individual liberty prevented any real constraint on big
business.

True, capitalism had the courts on their side, but
workers had the numbers. Not only did they organize
among themselves; they did so even more vigorously
than ever before. By 1920, union membership had risen

to five million, and the labor movement moved beyond its centrist demands, which had dominated the previous decades. In the 1890s, the voice of labor was Samuel Gompers, whose American Federation of Labor (AFL) endorsed anti-Black racism and segregated shops, and lobbied Congress to restrict immigration from China and Mexico. Gompers colluded with power as much as he could. By 1912, though, the voice of labor was the fiery midwesterner from Terre Haute, Indiana, Eugene V. Debs, who won an impressive nine hundred thousand votes for president when he ran as the Socialist Party candidate. A champion of women's suffrage and an antiracist in the Indiana state legislature, where he served for one term beginning in 1885, Debs evolved to socialism over time. This happened only after he read the writings of Karl Marx in prison, where he sat for six months. His crime: standing with over two hundred thousand Pullman railroad strikers in July 1894 who wouldn't accept drastic wage cuts of 30 percent, without a similar reduction of rent costs for the company housing in which they lived. "The solidarity of the working class is the salient force in the social transformation of which we behold the signs upon every hand," Debs said years later. "Nearer and nearer they are being drawn together in the bonds of unionism; clearer and clearer becomes their collective vision; greater and greater the power that throbs within them."[1]

Abolishing inequality doesn't happen spontaneously. For this to happen, you must organize. Labor has people power, but capitalism has repressive instruments. To crush the Pullman Strike, for instance, the sitting president, Grover Cleveland, equipped with an injunction from the federal courts, dispatched troops to Chicago. Twenty-six civilians died. This sort of violence was more common than you can imagine. When free-market evangelists tell you that capitalism has a great record, just remind them of the Homestead Strike of 1892, in which mercenary Pinkerton detectives, on behalf of the industrialist Andrew Carnegie's steel company, assaulted strikers from the Amalgamated Association of Iron and Steel Workers (AA). Or tell them about the Ludlow Massacre of 1914, when the private army of Rockefeller's Colorado Fuel and Iron Company opened fire upon striking mining families sleeping inside their tent colony. Thirteen women and children burned to death.

Debs understood that power doesn't crumble without a fight. There are two fronts upon which the war for economic equality has to be waged. The first is institutional. You need a robust political party to groom candidates for local and state government, and to push an agenda that breaks the long-standing monopoly of the two-party system. The second is a broad multiracial coalition of people. This was why Debs and William "Big Bill" Haywood founded the IWW (International Workers of the World) in 1905 in Chicago. The IWW endorsed spontaneous "wildcat" strikes without approval from leadership. Unlike the AFL, it rallied over one million unskilled industrial workers, including people of color, migrants, and women. At its peak, the IWW had over one hundred thousand members.

Yes, a broad base of support is indispensable. But you'll win concessions from management only if you keep up pressure that disrupts power's seamless flow. What's remarkable about the sixty-five thousand Seattle shipyard workers who participated in a work stoppage that ground the city to a halt in 1919 is that they organized a strike committee, which was responsible for deciding which services would be boycotted and which essential ones would continue. Sanitation workers collected wet trash, which was a grave public health risk. Firemen stayed on the job to prevent arson. Laundry workers remained open to keep people's clothing clean. Twenty-one makeshift dining halls serving thirty thousand meals a day were set up. This experiment was short-lived, however. The Seattle mayor sent in 2,400 police to shut it down.

But their example lived on when four hundred thousand railroad workers across the country went on strike in 1922, and fifteen thousand New Jersey textile workers did the same in 1926. Colorado coal miners followed suit in 1927. In 1933, over one million workers were involved in some kind of direct labor action. Newly inaugurated president, Democrat Franklin Roosevelt, had no choice but to cave and support labor demands. Consequently, he passed the National Industrial Recovery Act of 1933, which established a federal minimum wage and made unionization a right.

But when you win, you can't stop. You have to push harder. In May 1936, fourteen thousand San Francisco longshoremen defied their union leaders, who had colluded with management to weed out the younger, more militant and less-paid members among their ranks. The ILA (International Longshoremen's Association) negotiated a secret agreement that would have taken out the young workers, but, remembering Seattle in 1919, San Francisco longshoremen appealed to rank-and-file truck drivers and merchant marines to support their strike. The Teamsters Union agreed and stopped hauling cargo to and from the docks. The strike spread to 115 locals in San Francisco, and 130,000 people eventually joined. This was too radical a tactic for the AFL, which called the strikers communists. More than four thousand police and National Guard members were brought in to crush the strike, and vigilante groups followed suit with a concerted attack. But victory was close at hand. By 1935, Roosevelt had passed the Wagner Act and the Social Security Act. Soon, the Lochner Era came to a close, in 1937. That's when the Supreme Court, in *West Coast Hotel Co. v. Parrish*, overturned *Adkins* by upholding a state minimum wage law.

Nothing lasts forever. One step for labor precipitated a full-court assault from big business. The Taft-Hartley Act of 1947 banned spontaneous or wildcat strikes and mass protests from the grassroots without union leaders' approval. That was just the beginning of a series of measures that eroded labor's power. States soon began passing "right-to-work" legislation, which made unionization difficult. Years of chipping away culminated in the 2018 Supreme Court decision *Janus v. AFSCME*, in which a 5–4 conservative majority reversed long-standing precedent established in the *Abood* decision (1977). In *Janus*, the court argued that union dues violated the free speech clause of the First Amendment and made it constitutional for workers to opt out of paying union dues. This, even though the union would still represent them. Unions already stood little chance in terms of competing with corporations that had vast resources. *Janus* made it that much harder. The court used a similar principle in its *Citizen United* (2010) decision, which ruled that corporations had free speech rights and therefore could spend unlimited money on political campaigns.

Yes, pessimism makes sense. Look at our era of precarious flex work. Uber drivers are treated as private contractors, and retail employees at big-box stores are optimally scheduled for part-time hours to avoid paying full-time benefits. But be hopeful. Organizing is on the rise. Chicago teachers threatened to strike over being forced to resume in-person teaching during the COVID-19 pandemic, due to inadequate personal protective equipment and poorly ventilated, overcrowded classrooms. One hundred Washington State healthcare workers walked off their jobs in November 2020 because hospital administrators wouldn't reduce their twelve-hour shifts. Even Silicon Valley employees have gotten in on the action. Four hundred Google engineers, who met and held officer elections in secret, formed the Alphabet Workers Union in January 2021—an unprecedented achievement given the tech industry's hostility toward organized labor and its philosophy of growth at all costs. Democratic socialism, popularized by Vermont senator Bernie Sanders in 2016, is no longer the third rail of American politics. Join a union. Support labor rights. You have power in numbers. Remember that.

12

MAKE POLITICAL ART

Attacks on the arts have recently escalated. In his final year in office, Trump's proposed 2021 budget, entitled "Stopping Wasteful and Unnecessary Spending," aimed to cut $33 million from the National Endowment for the Humanities.[1] The COVID pandemic devastated culture in 2020 to the tune of a $15 billion loss. Museums shut down, plays were canceled, film festivals went virtual, and popular music venues shuttered their doors. Is it worth saving the arts? Good question, especially given so much upheaval over the past several years: Rising white supremacy. Ascendant nativism. Massive floods in the Midwest. Catastrophic wildfires in California. In light of all of this, you might wonder, What's the point of spending your time reading books or watching films when melancholy saturates the air we breathe? Actually, art is indispensable to political progress. Because art knows no rules, it expands them for you. What's familiar is gone. Your imagination is liberated. Art resonates emotionally. It stimulates your moral sensibility. A temporary refuge from the world isn't an escape. It sharpens your consciousness. It opens up your heart. It refreshes your spirit. Disaster is the best time for art. And art is at its best when confronting disaster.

This was the guiding belief of early-twentieth-century artists who confronted the Great Depression of the 1930s. To many, art must have seemed like an irrelevant distraction. Political corruption was rampant, and crowded cities and abandoned rural towns were characterized by obscene poverty and atrocious working conditions. Inequality was out of control. By the late 1920s, the tax rate on the rich, which, before World War I was 77 percent, fell to 25 percent. When the great speculative financial crash came to Wall Street in September 1929, the sitting president, Republican Herbert Hoover, dug deep into his boundless faith in rugged individualism. Preaching patience, Hoover wouldn't support any federal anti-poverty programs, believing that the Roaring Twenties would boom again soon.

But few writers, like workers in general, could wait for relief. They could barely afford to eat. For those who found work, it was easier to write melodramas that lacked dramatic punch and pulp romances divorced from the pressing issues of the day. But not all artists sold out. Turns out, provocative art is what the masses wanted.

The novelist Michael Gold, known as the dean of what became known as "proletariat literature," never saw writing as a realistic vocation when he was a kid. But he made his life—surrounded by Jewish Eastern European immigrants in the Lower East Side, where he grew up—the stuff of art. Gold never forgot his roots, even though he studied briefly at Harvard and then fled to Mexico to escape conscription in the First World War. His novel *Jews Without Money* (1930), part reverie, part autobiography, mostly a tale of lost dreams and frustrated expectations, became a surprise bestseller for the very reason critics thought it failed. The characters are flat, the plot is didactic, and the language is hard-boiled. Gold describes "mounds of pale stricken flesh tossing against an unreal city"[2] and offers thinly veiled metaphors like this one: "One steaming hot night I couldn't sleep for the bedbugs. They have a peculiar nauseating smell of their own; it is the smell of poverty. They crawl slowly and pompously, bloated with blood, and the touch and smell of these parasites wakens every nerve to disgust."

Irreverence is fashionable today, but Gold's fierce commitment to the possibility of revolutionary change is what readers admired back then and what we need more of today. The last lines of *Jews Without Money* don't treat hope in revolution with disdain but with a zeal that makes you feel like the end of misery is within reach: "O workers' Revolution, you brought hope to me, a lonely suicidal boy. . . . You will destroy the East Side when you come, and build there a garden for the human spirit."[3]

Gold didn't care about literary style. When he did, he preferred to be blunt. And why not? Getting readers to act might not happen through impeccably constructed sentences, but through inducing in them emotional responses. Gold must have learned this from Upton Sinclair, who encouraged him to begin his magazine, *New Masses* (1926–1948). By the time they met, Sinclair was an aspiring socialist politician running unsuccessfully for Congress. But in 1906, he was a muckraking journalist turned novelist on a lark. This, when the editor of a socialist magazine edited by midwestern populists, *Appeal to Reason*, which had over five hundred thousand subscribers, gave Sinclair five hundred dollars to expose the horrors of the US meatpacking industry. The novel that emerged after seven weeks of intensive interviews,

The Jungle (1906), depicted the conditions endured by Chicago's immigrant meat workers, who made food that mixed human and rodent remains in unimaginably filthy factories.

As a child, Sinclair found that his sense of humor saved him. The son of a traveling salesman, he escaped the poorhouse in New York by financing his own education at City College through joke books he wrote as a teen. But nothing was funny about *The Jungle*. That's why it had an impact Sinclair never anticipated. "I aimed for the public's heart and hit it in the stomach," he remarked.[4] Sinclair left an indelible mark. On first reading it, the sitting president, Teddy Roosevelt, thought the book was sensational fiction. But after dispatching secret investigators to observe labor practices at meatpacking plants, he realized that Sinclair's depiction was tame compared to the real thing. After the ensuing public outcry, Congress regulated the production of food through the Meat Inspection Act and the Pure Food and Drug Act of 1906.

The new regulatory regime was only an incremental step toward reforming capitalism. But its lesson is clear: art can change politics. This is what the photographer Dorothea Lange set out to do when she was given a job photographing migrant farmworkers in

California through FDR's Works Progress Administration. The WPA, established in 1936, employed thousands of out-of-work painters, writers, and musicians. Lange, born in 1895, began as an out-of-touch portrait photographer of the well-to-do in San Francisco. But as the Depression lengthened, her first marriage crumbled, and the art market disintegrated, Lange left her comfortable private studio and was reborn in the streets. This is where she first took snapshots of people sleeping on sidewalks and of labor uprisings at the barricade. She left her first husband and remarried the University of California, Berkeley, economist Paul Taylor, who was researching Mexican immigration. Together, they chronicled the wreckage of the Dust Bowl.

When she and Taylor set foot in the California fields, Lange was shocked to find laborers, after a long day of digging potatoes and picking cotton, "camped in an open field, without shelter of any kind. Mother pregnant, with 5 starving children . . . eating green onions, raw, and that was all they had."[5] She resolved to give flesh to the abstraction of poverty through what still remains the iconic image of the era, the unforgettable *Migrant Mother* (1936). The photo is of a thirty-two-year-old mother, looking pensively into the distance, with two of her seven children burying their faces in her neck. Here and elsewhere, Lange stressed the human will against the dehumanized system that crushes it. In her photographs, images of laborers' improvised homes, tents made of cardboard and linoleum, are juxtaposed against a highly organized agricultural system, of fields plowed by depersonalizing tractors.

Beyond helping to pay the bills, Lange's photographs had a profound cultural legacy. They were the biggest influence on a writer born in Salinas Valley, California, who would eventually win the Nobel Prize in 1962. His best-selling novel *The Grapes of Wrath* (1939), which became a popular film, would shape American consciousness: John Steinbeck. While in the Mexican countryside on set for a film he wrote, *The Forgotten Village* (1941), he was accompanied by a rising Black novelist, Richard Wright, whose book *Native Son* (1940) had caused a national stir a year earlier. Wright created an antihero, Bigger Thomas, a young Black man who is ensnared in a racist-capitalist system in the South Side of Chicago, which enrages and then destroys him. Though the story of Bigger shocked white liberals, Wright's greatest achievement was to inspire a new crop of Black artists. What struck young writers like James Baldwin, Margaret Walker, and Ralph Ellison when they first encountered Wright's fiction, and who were supported by his generosity, was that Wright's unfiltered depiction of Bigger's rage felt authentic. Wright drew from his own life—his childhood in Mississippi, where lynching was part of the landscape, and his experience in Illinois, where he was among the first Black writers to work for the WPA, in 1935.

Wright's Bigger Thomas didn't fit the caricature of Black forgiveness, made famous in Harriet Beecher Stowe's *Uncle Tom's Cabin* (1852), or that of Black passivity in *Gone with the Wind* (1939). Wright wouldn't stand for polite white liberalism that was toothless in its desire for moderation, if not racist behind its veneer, because he was a radical. Wright was a card-carrying member of the Communist Party and a book reviewer for the political journal that Gold edited, *New Masses*. But the goal of Wright's art, more so than anything else, was to radicalize readers' perceptions. You see this in the remarkable *12 Million Black Voices* (1941), an extended lyric essay on Black life during the Great Depression, accompanied by ninety Farm Security Administration photos curated by Edwin Rosskam.

Lange let her images speak for themselves. But Wright's words describing the gazes, movements, and expressions of Black sharecroppers, maids, dancers, and waiters reorient the reader's perspective of the US:

"What we want, what we represent, what we endure is what *is*," Wright writes. "If we black folk perish, America will perish."[6] Black resistance in the face of catastrophic white racism is what Wright calls a "mirror" that he forces the nation to confront directly.

Art is, and has always been, a tool for disorientation. Good. Disorientation is what's demanded in times of crisis. The right kind. Find art that makes you feel solidarity with those you'd least expect. To find courage yourself. To see anew. To be rejuvenated. In one of the darkest periods in American history, artists were adamant about art's revolutionary potential. We have every reason to believe too.

13

PAINT A BLOODY PICTURE

The powerful prefer to keep politically caused cruelty hidden from public view. When you're told to stop discussing the hundreds of thousands of COVID-19 deaths even if it's because of the Trump administration's malfeasance, there are echoes of history. Don't name the US soldiers killed during the Iraq War from 2003 to 2011 to promote Bush's neoconservative platform of spreading democracy abroad. Don't show on television body bags filled with young kids drafted to limit the spread of Soviet communism during the Vietnam War in the 1960s. Let's be clear: censoring cruelty censors vibrant opposition. So, paint a picture of disaster in all its bloody detail. When you do this, you not only create a more accurate historical record, but you make it hard for others to look away. In the face of the truth, they can't be deluded by the fantasy that everything is alright, that things aren't that bad. Now they have to confront what disaster does to people. Because cruelty doesn't impact everyone in the same way, we must take into account the perspective of those who live it.

The lesson of antinuclear activists in the 1940s is that they roused public sentiment by scandalizing their audience. They forced them, whether they liked it or not, to confront what was far away. No text was more successful in this endeavor than the 31,000-word article "Hiroshima" by the Pulitzer Prize–winning novelist who moonlighted as a reporter, John Hersey. First published in the *New Yorker* on August 31, 1946, the book version, *Hiroshima*, appeared a year after the B-29 bomber *Enola Gay*, on the order of President Harry S. Truman during the Second World War, dropped a nuclear bomb and destroyed five square miles of the industrial city of Hiroshima, Japan. One-third of the city's population, one hundred thousand, were murdered.

No publication in the twentieth-century United States, and certainly none since, had as much of an impact on national consciousness. The entire *New Yorker* print run of three hundred thousand—in which Hiroshima, contrary to the magazine's usual format, represented the content of an entire issue—sold out immediately. ABC

Radio read the essay live over four nights. After it was published as a book, by Knopf, it received countless positive reviews and book club selections.

What accounted for *Hiroshima*'s unprecedented success? By meticulously detailing the lives of six survivors, and the wreckage of the bomb, Hersey undercut official US government narratives that had emphasized the strategic necessity of forcing imperial Japan's surrender. Within days of the bombing, the US military began a concerted propaganda campaign, releasing information to willing reporters in magazines like *Time* and *Life* that described Hiroshima as a military target, emphasizing the damage done to buildings, and implying that, though the choice of weapon was new and unique, the bombing was part of ordinary protocols. This idea was perpetuated in the best-selling book *Dawn Over Zero* (1946), by *New York Times* science reporter William Laurence, who was the official reporter for the Manhattan Project and the only journalist who witnessed the Nagasaki bombing firsthand.

Hersey wouldn't allow the disaster to be told from the perspective of the perpetrators, who gave us a plane's-eye view, thousands of feet in the air. In Hersey's telling, after an apocalyptic "tremendous flash of light,"[1] Hiroshima is transformed from a paradise of commerce into a hellscape. The mushroom cloud of smoke is pierced by a "shower of tiles [that] pommeled" people, and the ground opens to become a crypt in which men, women, and children are buried alive without warning. Hersey forces readers to think about how what was once mundane has transformed into a waking nightmare: in a hospital, "heavy partitions and ceilings had fallen on patients, beds had overturned, windows had blown in and cut people, blood was spattered on the walls and floors, instruments were everywhere, many of the patients were running about screaming, many more lay dead." You think about how the children, many of whom were barely able to talk or walk, were out in the street with "nothing on but underpants." Imagine you were part of a procession of mourners, who were barely upright as they hobbled toward their own death, their bodies collapsing upon themselves and exploding in public, forming a grotesque mass. "Wounded people supported maimed people; disfigured families leaned together," Hersey writes. "Many people were vomiting. A tremendous number of schoolgirls . . . crept into the hospital."[2]

So after you've read *Hiroshima*, you don't need Hersey to understand that those who survive only survive in the literal sense. Their lives are distant memories of what they once were. One survivor is disabled, the other is destitute, and still another is living in a hospital. One can't work, another knows the hospital in which he worked won't be rebuilt, and another won't return to the smashed church where he worshiped for years. Before reading *Hiroshima* and being exposed to US propaganda, you may have thought Truman had no choice. But now you question this view: Was there really no other way? Was it justified? War is no longer an abstraction to be addressed through theories of rational choice, strategic alliances, and geopolitical maneuvers. War has a face. Ask yourself: Can you accept its costs?

Hersey's example is as relevant now as ever. Urge journalists to detail the violence inflicted upon villagers in Afghanistan who are the collateral damage of US drone strikes. In 2019, photojournalist Stefanie Glinski visited the Achin district community, where a US strike—one of 4,251 in that year alone—intended to target ISIS fighters killed thirty pine nut farmers and injured forty more instead. Glinski supplements her photographs of homes in rubble with survivors' testimony. Don't allow anyone to say such attacks are, regretfully, the cost of pursuing the US war on terror. Against the words of a US colonel whose language cloaks the human damage of the violence—"We are aware of allegations of the death of non-combatants and are working with local officials to determine the facts"—Glinski uses the words of a thirty-five-year-old woman, whose husband was killed, recalling how the strike began as the farmers had "completed their first days of work. We've heard planes circle above the village and in the distance, we've been hearing explosions."[3]

Don't fall into the trap of debating a policy's efficacy for national security. Consider the consequences on the people who will pay the price for your comfort. Don't ask which immigration law best deters migrants from arriving on US shores but instead ask, What are the deleterious psychological effects upon young refugee children escaping gang warfare in El Salvador and Guatemala, who are forcibly separated from their parents by ICE agents in Texas at the US-Mexico border? Jessica Goodkind, a sociologist at the University of New Mexico, did that and was surprised to find that "family separation was on par with beating and torture in terms of its relationship to mental health.... It is one of the driving factors that creates psychological distress."[4] Atrocities hidden from view abet the perpetuation of future atrocities. The light of truth is the best disinfectant for the virus of moral apathy that renders citizens immobile in the face of injustice.

14

POLITICIZE GRIEF

Privatizing disaster is common. Sometimes, we want to flee politics because it's just so overwhelming. That's why, in September 2020, Democratic vice presidential candidate Kamala Harris was commended when she took time out of her hectic campaign schedule to go to Milwaukee. Behind closed doors, with no media present, Harris met with the family of the twenty-nine-year-old Black man, Jacob Blake. Blake was paralyzed by white police officers in Kenosha, Wisconsin, who shot him seven times in the back at point-blank range as he reached into the dashboard of his parked car. As Harris told reporters later, she simply wanted to "express concern for their well-being and of course, for their brother and their son's well-being and to let them know that they have support."[1]

Deep within your heart, you agree with Harris's motives. You want to empathize with victims of police violence, to say how sorry you feel for what they're going through. To grieve with them. But some disasters aren't entirely personal. The reason we hear about them in the first place is because they're not unique. We know that they're part of a broader pattern. The shooting of Jacob Blake was one of hundreds of instances in which Black people are shot by police every year in the US. So, make tragedy unforgettable for those who want to move on. Make collective action defeat individual apathy. Grieve politically.

The clearest expression of this is seen in the life of Mamie Till-Mobley. You may not know her story, but she's one of the heroes in US history. Her fourteen-year-old Black son, Emmett, was visiting relatives in Money, Mississippi, in August 1955 when he was lynched by two white supremacists. On a hot summer afternoon, Emmett was falsely accused of whistling at a white woman, Carolyn Bryant, who owned a grocery store. Emmett's body, bruised and beaten, pierced with a bullet and a seventy pound cotton gin tied around his neck as an anchor, was later found deep in the Tallahatchie River. Local white officials wanted to cover up the murder so they could continue to say that Jim Crow was perfectly civilized. Mamie Till, however, wouldn't allow them to control the public narrative. She demanded that her boy's body be flown to his hometown, Chicago, for a public burial. The funeral director, A. A. Raynor, warned her to keep the casket shut, for the sake of not having to relive the trauma. But she demanded that it stay open, saying she would pry it open with her own bare hands. "I was putting him back together again," Till recalled.[2]

Mamie politicized her grief. She wasn't swallowed whole by its overwhelming force. Young Emmett's brutalized body, she wants the world to see, is proof of what racism does to its innocent victims. Jim Crow isn't simply about being denied a good seat at the local movie theater. It's not merely being forced to sit in the back of the bus. Jim Crow is a bloodthirsty, maniacal expression of dehumanization that knows no boundaries. This is the loud message that Mamie shared with the one hundred thousand people who attended the open-casket burial at the Roberts Temple Church of God in Christ in Chicago. Many of them fainted and were aided by nurses, who were on call to provide care. Millions more saw a photograph of Emmett's precious body, destroyed by white terror in the now iconic picture published in *Jet* magazine and the *Chicago Defender*. "I was not going quietly," Till explained. "They had to see what I had seen. The whole nation had to bear witness to this."[3]

Mamie didn't privatize her pain. Grieving in public, she knew, creates a community to work through grief collectively.

Despite overwhelming evidence pointing to their guilt, the two white men who lynched Emmett were acquitted after an all-white jury deliberated for less than an hour. But Jim Crow justice didn't win following the "not guilty" verdict. On November 27, 1955, the Black civil rights activist Dr. T. R. M. Howard, remembering Mamie Till's labor of love, delivered a speech he had given many times over the past months about the details of Emmett's lynching. In it he gave the names of the white perpetrators and the blow-by-blow details of what was known about the case at that point. That night, Howard spoke at the Dexter Avenue Baptist Church in Montgomery, Alabama, whose new pastor was a twenty-six-year-old with a Boston University PhD in theology, Martin Luther King Jr. A forty-two-year-old seamstress was also attending Howard's speech. Her name was Rosa Parks. Four days later, on December 1, after a long and tiring day of work, she would refuse to sit in the back of a segregated bus, sparking what became 381 days of the Montgomery bus boycott, the most successful freedom struggle in US history. Four months later, Howard spoke to a crowd of three thousand in

Chicago, relaying King's message from the streets of Montgomery, where the battle was well underway. "Tell the folks in Chicago," King said, "we have enlisted in this fight for the duration."[4]

Tears help you process what might seem unbearable, but they can also be the source of transformative social work. And this goes well beyond our own feelings. President Barack Obama, known for his public composure, politicized grief in the most positive way when, on June 26, 2015, he gave an impassioned eulogy a week after the Charleston massacre, when a white supremacist murdered nine Black parishioners at an AME church in South Carolina. Speaking at the College of Charleston for one of the murdered, the Reverend Clementa Pinckney, Obama poignantly denounced the scourge of racial inequality in the city. Charleston, he declares, is "a place still wracked by poverty and inadequate schools; a place where children can still go hungry and the sick can go without treatment," and he singled out the "unique mayhem that gun violence inflicts upon this nation."[5] In March 2018, one month after teenagers saw seventeen of their classmates gunned down by another one of their classmates at Marjorie Stoneman Douglas High School in Parkland, Florida, three thousand marched onto the school's football field in protest. They were part of a nationwide school walkout. That same day, students at Baltimore Polytechnic staged a "lie-in," where they lay motionless on the ground for seventeen minutes— each minute symbolizing one of the Parkland children murdered. Their goal: gun control. Critics say pray; don't march. Make a vigil; don't propose legislation. But the students were in good company. As a Black mother once showed the world, tragedy can be the best time for politics. That's when the world is watching. Grab their attention.

15

CREATE A COUNTERCULTURE

Dread fills the air we breathe. The apocalyptic wildfires that spread throughout California in 2020 and color the San Francisco skyline orange, after bone-dry conditions, spur feelings of climate grief, because the planet's warming temperatures will make it uninhabitable for humans by the end of the century. College students no longer assume when they graduate that they'll have a solid career that will take them into retirement. They wonder if they'll find enough gig work to offset the massive student debt they have accrued to pay for their education. The escalating use of surveillance capitalism makes the right to privacy seem like a relic of a distant era. One wonders whether dissent is the next casualty in our dystopian future.

Dread isn't new. It's as American as the crises to which it's a response. Every generation battles the fear of total annihilation. The solution isn't to take a Pollyannaish attitude, to say that everything, ultimately, will be okay if we wait it out. It's to create a counterculture opposed to what's corrosive in the mainstream. A culture of values that diminish the flames of exploitation.

This is what American youth did in the 1960s in a moment, like ours, defined by social upheaval. The Vietnam War left thousands of Americans and millions of Vietnamese dead. After the nationally televised draft lottery, organized by the Nixon administration, on December 1, 1969, there seemed to be little optimism for an end in sight. There was also the new postwar capitalism, symbolized by a traditional middle-class family that lived in places like a lily-white suburb of Poughkeepsie. Men in suits headed to their corporate jobs at advertising agencies on Madison Avenue. Women stayed home to care for the kids. On a positive note, the Black freedom struggle, then in its second decade, was finally adding political victories with the Civil Rights Act of 1964 and the Voting Rights Act of 1965. But if white people barely tolerated the nonviolent civil disobedience of a Martin Luther King in Birmingham, Alabama, in the face of segregationist sheriffs in June 1963, they were petrified of the increasing militancy of activists like Huey Newton and the Black Panther Party's rhetoric of self-defense in Oakland, California, in 1966.

In these turbulent times, American youth faced a stark choice: follow in their parents' footsteps or opt out and make their own path. The first choice was comfortable, the second alienating. But alienation is lessened by love. So they formed a beloved community. San Francisco's Haight-Ashbury district was the locus of the Summer of Love of 1967, which saw one hundred thousand hippies flock to the city's parks.

The writings of the 1950s Beat Generation were their spiritual guide. Being beaten down by society can be a rallying cry for revolution. In between classes on college campuses across the nation, lying on grassy campuses before class, students read out loud the elegiac poetry of their disheveled, bespectacled Jesus, Allen Ginsberg. In coffee shops and dive bars on New York City's Bleecker Street, they memorized passages from *On the Road*, by Ginsberg's Columbia University friend and classmate Jack Kerouac. They wanted to get lost and not found. Life, they believed, should be a psychedelic trip of cut-ups—with beginnings, middles, and ends out of order. This was the stream-of-consciousness style pioneered by William S. Burroughs, most notably in his novel *Naked Lunch* (1959).

American culture needs to be reformed. This, at least, is what attendees of the 1967 Human Be-In at San

Francisco's Golden Gate Park believed. They wore hand-made tie-dye shirts and bell-bottom pants. Men and women grew out their hair. They performed avant-garde folk and psychedelic rock. Ate vegetarian and practiced yoga. And chanted "Make Love, Not War!"

Irreverence against authority wasn't only evident in the counterculture's style; it was part of their politics. The best example is the Diggers. Formed in 1966, they gave away free food to the unsheltered every afternoon at the Fell Street Panhandle in San Francisco. They later expanded their mutual aid to include free bus rides, clothing, housing, medical care, and legal services. Beyond this direct work, the Diggers had an impact upon the Yippies (members of the Youth International Party), which was officially founded by the prankster Abbie Hoffman on New Year's Eve 1967 and combined guerrilla street theater and political satire to attack symbols of American power. Hoffman is best remembered for, along with twenty co-conspirators, dropping a hundred dollar bills from the balcony of the New York Stock Exchange on August 24, 1967. They watched with delight when the male brokers stopped their trading on a dime to catch as many bills as possible as they slowly floated toward the exchange floor. Hoffman's goal, "the death of money," was as important for drawing media attention as it was for infusing a sense of playfulness into the antiwar movement. Up until that point, the movement was no fun. It was solemn as ever—with almost five hundred thousand US soldiers deployed in Vietnam, and many more to come.

Shortly after this prank, Hoffman, along with Allen Ginsberg, organized another one: a march of thousands to levitate and exorcise the Pentagon of evil, on October 21, 1967. This came just days after the bloody Battle of Ong Thanh, in which sixty-four Americans were killed. Hoffman wasn't done. His most memorable act came during the Democratic National Convention in August 1968, months after Martin Luther King was gunned down in Memphis and presumptive Democratic presidential candidate, Bobby Kennedy, met the same fate in the Ambassador Hotel in Los Angeles. In Grant Park in Chicago, Hoffman and the Yippies, despite being denied a protest permit by Mayor Richard Daley, nominated a mock 145-pound pig (Pigasus) for president. Humor can be disarming, welcoming in bystanders, telling them that activism can be joyful. But not all will be amused. Chicago police at Grant Park were disgusted and increasingly grew impatient. Then things turned ugly when a man at the protest lowered an American flag on a flagpole. On August 28, after a tense back-and-forth of shouting with Chicago police, hundreds were beaten and gassed—all of it caught on camera and broadcast. Hoffman and six more, together known as the Chicago Seven, were indicted for inciting a riot. During the trial, in September 1969, Hoffman did what he was good at: making a mockery of vaunted institutions. He showed up in black judicial robes, underneath which was a Chicago police uniform. He read poetry and chanted Hare Krishna devotionals, for which he—along with the others—was charged with contempt of the court. For this, he was given a two-year prison sentence, which, upon appeal, was overturned in 1970.

Not everyone was amused with Hoffman's antics. Not middle-class white Americans who saw Hoffman embodying everything wrong with the longhairs. They'd had enough. As part of the so-called silent majority, they put Republican Richard Nixon, and his strongman "law and order" message, into power in 1968. Before long, the US was in the midst of a right-wing reaction against everything Hoffman and the counterculture fought for.

Knowing what happened, you might be tempted to say it wasn't worth it. But who's to say that without these spectacles, corporate greed would still be headline news on CBS or part of editorials in the *New York Times* in the late 1960s? Would young people beyond the major metropolises—in places like Nebraska, Wisconsin, Oklahoma, and Mississippi—still have heated, if not irreparable breaks, with their parents at the dinner table over the future of the nation? Sure, the 1960s were a divisive time. But without the counterculture's revealing of deep social fault lines just beneath the surface, would there have been the public outcry that ultimately washed Nixon out of office in 1974 after the Watergate scandal and put an end to the Vietnam War in 1975?

Maybe. Who knows? But one thing is for sure. The counterculture fundamentally changed the conversation about what's worthwhile. And sometimes making a scene on your own terms is the only way to confront paralyzing dread. This makes you feel less alone. You're part of a community. Your values are represented—not those of your parents. That's how it should be. It's your future. Not theirs.

16

REVOLUTIONIZE IDENTITY

Disaster makes us seek out self-preservation. When threats to our identity loom large, we make concessions to protect ourselves. When we feel unsafe, it's easier to stay hidden in the shadows, to temporarily withdraw so we can regroup. This, in fact, is what conservatives desire. Consider how immediately after the #MeToo movement in 2017 placed a glaring spotlight on women's experience of sexual violence and harassment in the workplace, there was a swift backlash. Employers retaliated by firing survivors who spoke up about assault in the hospitality and service industry where wages are low. Being vocal has enormous costs. Some of the women who weren't silent were blacklisted from industries in which they'd worked for decades. Others had their cases summarily dismissed in court by judges citing insufficient evidence.[1]

Surveying the dramatic rise of retaliation claims filed with the Equal Employment Opportunity Commission a year after #MeToo came to national prominence, a *Vox* article declared, "Whether or not the past year has led to cultural change, one thing hasn't changed: For working-class people, speaking out still means risking their job."[2] But there's a way to resist. Forge a new identity. Make society into what you want it to be, rather than what it wants you to be. Advocate for revolutionary transformation when you're told to be quiet. This gives you a sense of power that anything's possible. Be vocal about what you won't tolerate. This creates a new vocabulary of justice in which silence doesn't rule. You're not conforming to rules that you reject. You're asserting your own.

This is the lesson of feminists excluded from the prevailing view of women's liberation. The flurry of reforms in the 1970s heartened second-wave white middle-class feminists like Betty Friedan, who wrote the best-selling *The Feminine Mystique* (1963) and cofounded the National Organization for Women (NOW) in 1966. In 1972, Title IX of the Education Amendments barred federal funding to colleges that discriminated against women. The 1974 Equal Credit Opportunity Act made it illegal for banks to deny mortgages to women.

Throughout the late 1960s, divorce laws in states became less draconian, and the wage gap between men and women was not as wide as before.

But sometimes reforms conceal more than they fix. They patch up a broken system by giving it the veneer of progress. Take for example the state law passed in Colorado in 1967 that made abortion legal but created a set of onerous conditions that proved hard to meet for many women wishing to terminate unwanted pregnancies. The new rule was especially devastating for the poor. Women were required to provide written consent from two doctors and a hospital committee, and they needed to ensure that the low-risk procedure would be performed in a costly inpatient hospital setting.

When the New York State Legislative Committee on Public Health was debating its own abortion reform proposal on February 13, 1969, before a room of fifteen expert witnesses—fourteen men and one nun—they expected to be praised. But they were wrong. The cofounder of the radical feminist outfit Redstockings, a *Village Voice* essayist, and the first pop music critic for the *New Yorker*, Ellen Willis, the daughter of a New York City Police Department lieutenant, along with several others, broke away from the NOW members picketing outside the statehouse. They stormed the chamber, stood up, without sanction, and began to shout, "Let's hear from the real experts—women!"[3]

New York legislators begged them to "act like ladies," but to no avail. The next day, the New York tabloid the *Daily News* ran a front-page headline saying, "Gals KO Abortion Hearing." Remember: those whose freedoms are at stake in any policy must be heard. And to be heard, you sometimes have no choice but to smash institutions that prevent you from speaking, even if these institutions are rooted in society and won't go quietly into the night. This is why another Redstockings cofounder, the Canadian-born, St. Louis-raised twenty-five-year-old no-nonsense Shulamith Firestone, argued in *The Dialectic of Sex* (1970) that women shouldn't have children. Women's domestic caregiving allows men to work outside the home and capitalism to function freely, Firestone writes.

Two years earlier, Firestone organized New York Radical Women (NYRW). She had just moved to the city after completing her degree in painting from the Art Institute of Chicago. NYRW and Firestone made art into politics on September 7, 1968, when she, along with more than four hundred NYRW members, traveling from as far as Boston and Florida, staged a protest of the forty-second Miss America Pageant on the boardwalk of Atlantic City. They threw into the trash all kinds of things—mops, heels, makeup, old copies of *Cosmopolitan* forced upon them by their husbands and sons. These common household objects and beauty supplies they called "instruments of feminine torture."

Queer feminists, however, had to fight on two fronts: against die-hard misogynists and against liberals concerned with making feminism socially palatable. Betty Friedan called lesbians within the movement the "lavender menace." The professional guidebook for psychiatry, *The Diagnostic and Statistical Manual of Mental Disorders (DSM)*, labeled homosexuality a mental illness until 1973, when it was changed to a "sexual orientation disturbance," though it did not remove homosexuality as a disorder until 1987. But queer feminists wouldn't allow homophobia to define who they were and what they did. Karla Jay, the Brooklyn-born, conservative-Jewish-raised feminist, abandoned her insulated and traditional upbringing when she came out as a lesbian and become involved with Students for a Democratic Society at Columbia University, where she completed her undergraduate degree in French in 1968. Eventually, Jay soured on the New Left's male leaders, whose latent authoritarianism stood in stark contrast to the egalitarian consciousness-raising group associated with Redstockings, which she joined in 1969.

That same year, Jay was galvanized by the six days of defiant clashes between hundreds of Greenwich Village's gay community and the NYPD along Christopher Street after cops raided a gay bar, the Stonewall Inn, beginning in the early morning hours of June 28. The militant organization that Jay cofounded in the aftermath, the Gay Liberation Front (GLF), was done playing nice. "Do you think homosexuals are revolting?" GLF flyers, posted across the East Village's community centers and clubs, asked rhetorically. "You bet your sweet ass we are."[4] The GLF renounced assimilationism, which involved normalizing gay people as good neighbors and productive coworkers.

The battle, Jay believed, needed to be taken to one's allies. That's why she, along with several others, hijacked the Second Congress to Unite Women on May 1, 1970, in New York. Dressed in lavender shirts, they cut the lights, seized the microphones, and stormed the stage with signs that said "Take a lesbian to lunch" and "Women's liberation is a lesbian plot." The satire, playing on homophobic fears, and calling into question the farce of women's unity, was at its heart an act of coming out. Coming out is about forming a public identity not governed by the master's rules. That's how shame is erased. And distinctions between what is normal and what isn't are exploded.

Both Redstockings and the GLF expressed solidarity with the Black freedom struggle, although few of its members were women of color. Unlike white women activists, Black women had a history of strategizing against both racism and sexism. Twenty miles north of Manhattan, in Mount Vernon, the Black Women's Liberation Movement, composed of working women of color, issued a widely circulated document, "Statement on Birth Control" (1968). The statement connected reproductive rights to welfare, housing, and education rights.

But reproductive freedom, for Black feminists, was also a struggle against something that affluent white women rarely faced: forced sterilization. In the 1970s, compulsory sterilization was a common occurrence for Black women across the United States. Moreover, the measure was being embraced for punitive purposes in the state capitols of Louisiana, Maryland, California, Connecticut, Delaware, and Virginia. In 1971, for instance, a Republican state legislator in South Carolina,

Lucius Porth, endorsed a law that made welfare recipients with two children choose between renouncing public assistance or being forcibly sterilized.[5]

This horrific decision, however, wasn't given to a twelve-year-old Black child, Minnie Lee Relf. Deemed mentally incompetent by Alabama caseworkers in 1973, Relf underwent tubal ligation without her family's consent at a federally funded family planning clinic in the birthplace of the civil rights movement: Montgomery, Alabama.[6] The fight for abortion is also a fight against sterilization, so said the statement of the Third World Women's Workshop held in Michigan in 1971, "because the lack of legal abortion has been used for years to force women to undergo sterilization."[7]

This feminist legacy lives on. Conservatives may be emboldened by Trump's appointment of activist judges handpicked by the Federalist Society, like Neil Gorsuch, Brett Kavanaugh, and Amy Coney Barrett to the US Supreme Court. Now they have a 6–3 supermajority, but young activists aren't backing down. Instead of staying silent, they're turning the tables on the enemies of freedom. Without question, women's reproductive rights, and especially *Roe v. Wade*, are in serious doubt. But rather than concede ground to the right—and say, for instance, that abortion should only be the last means available to address unwanted pregnancies—reproductive justice activists insist that a women's right to choose is a matter of both racial and economic justice.

Similarly, as some moderates try to preserve the right to gay marriage affirmed by the Supreme Court in *Obergefell v. Hodges* (2015), LGBTQ activists question whether marriage is a just institution, and whether as a society, this should be the family structure we endorse. These activists transform their identities into revolutionary forces. It's not just for them, but for all of us. If patriarchy is destroyed, we can be freer than we imagined.

MAKE AN ANGRY SPECTACLE

An epidemic of anger, fueled by hyperpolarization, is seen as one of the greatest disasters afflicting US democracy. As one author recently put it, "Anger causes Americans to adopt attitudes that run contrary to the democratic ideals of the nation. . . . It makes Americans see supporters of the opposing political party as less intelligent than themselves. Arguably more harmful for democracy, anger also makes people see supporters of the opposing political party as a threat to the country's well-being."[1] A nation this divided, we're constantly told, needs cooler heads to prevail. Delete the nasty tweets and emotionally charged viral videos. Turn down the temperature of your rhetoric.

But a politics without spectacle can't be a contentious politics, which is what's necessary to get those in power to listen. When disaster strikes, raw emotion gets noticed. Your concerns are taken more seriously, rather than swept under the rug. An angry public spectacle stages your grievances and demands, especially when they're dismissed as unserious. And yet, just because you're angry doesn't mean you're violent. All successful nonviolent civil disobedience movements are, in fact, marked by righteous indignation. Orchestrating an emotionally charged performance is good theater and good politics. It draws in onlookers. This is something that methodical, measured persuasion within boardrooms or classrooms can't do. Here's how anger can be provocative in the best possible sense. It can activate a community's moral compass and make citizens act.

In the 1980s, anger was a lifeline for the gay liberation movement. Its goal? To combat homophobic public policies. A mixture of silence and disgust defined the US government's position toward the AIDS epidemic decimating gay men. As the disease was killing tens of thousands across the country, and the virus that caused it was infecting hundreds of thousands, Republican president Ronald Reagan's administration said nothing. The administration only began to quietly fund AIDS research in 1983, two years after the disease was becoming impossible to ignore. And throughout the decade, Reagan continued to cut the negligible amount he did allocate, even as the crisis accelerated. Reagan himself, eager to court the support of the increasingly powerful antigay Christian Right, led by Jerry Falwell and Pat Robertson, which formed his core electoral base, said nothing publicly about AIDS until an April 2, 1987, speech on the matter. By then, almost fifty thousand Americans had died. As late as 1984, Reagan's press secretary, Larry Speakes, would have a good laugh with reporters, joking at a press conference that Reagan had not "expressed concern" about what some were calling the "gay plague."[2]

Not everyone thought AIDS was funny. Certainly not a new organization, ACT UP (AIDS Coalition to Unleash Power), which held its first meeting in New York City at the Gay and Lesbian Community Center in Greenwich Village in March 1987. Soon, it would have chapters in Chicago and San Francisco. If you attended an ACT UP meeting, you would see a diverse group— men, women, old, young, gay, Black, white—strategizing how best to make the nation awaken to the disaster. Tired of the bland rhetoric of inclusivity and milquetoast appeals to sameness, activists at the first New York meeting spoke about changing their focus from "Gay Pride" to "Gay Rage." Make no mistake, ACT UP were partisans of love. Many of the queer men and women who went to meetings multiple times a week would hug, kiss, joke, sit on each other's laps, flirt with one another.

Indeed, ACT UP meetings were a way of forging solidarity and validating desires denigrated in public.

But if love is indispensable in making you feel like you're worth fighting for, anger is what ups the ante about the utter seriousness of your convictions. Anger draws a line in the sand for your enemies, telling them you won't be mistreated. On the weekend of October 11, 1988, equipped with posters featuring a pink triangle and below it the text "Silence = Death," over one thousand ACT UP activists went to Washington, DC, and surrounded FDA (Food and Drug Administration) headquarters, which they called the "Federal Death Administration." They protested the slow pace at which FDA was approving experimental anti-HIV drugs for general use. Their rally was a response to an event being held the same weekend in DC: the Names Project AIDS Memorial Quilt was unfurled on the National Mall, to celebrate and mourn the lives lost to the epidemic. ACT UP stood in solidarity with the Names Project's unabashed championing of LGBTQ rights, though they disagreed with their tactic of being as palatable as possible for straight people. As ACT UP put it in leaflets they circulated around DC: "SHOW YOUR ANGER TO THE PEOPLE WHO HELPED MAKE THE QUILT POSSIBLE: OUR GOVERNMENT..."

Before this Quilt grows any larger, turn your grief into anger. Turn anger into action. TURN THE POWER OF THE QUILT INTO ACTION."[3]

Several years later, on October 11, 1992, at 1:00 p.m., at the tail end of the administration of Reagan's successor, Republican George H. W. Bush, ACT UP went further. They brought the AIDS Quilt to life in a shocking way through a political funeral. Bush, unlike Reagan, acknowledged AIDS, but he still cut AIDS research funding and safe sex education in public schools. In response, ACT UP marched in a solemn procession toward the White House, with activists holding the ashes of dead lovers, friends, and family, people with whom they had real connections and memories, and who were now gone because of government neglect. There were no loudspeakers from which to amplify bold talking points. No podiums from which to give celebrities a platform. Instead, activists hurled their anonymous bodies and pitched their screams toward the White House fence. Some of them scaled the fence, others heaved the ashes of the dead over it and onto the lawn, darkening the pristine green with the gray of indignation.

Two weeks later, just before the 1992 presidential election, the body of ACT UP/NY member Mark Fisher was carried in an open casket for onlookers to bear witness. The funeral march was set to the pulse of a single drum reverberating among the skyscrapers, beginning from Jackson Memorial Church and ending at George H. W. Bush's Manhattan reelection headquarters. As one of the funeral's organizers, Eric Sawyer, put it, the march was about ushering forth "the death of the Bush presidency. We knew his evil neglect of people with AIDS, and his hatred of LGBTQ+ people would bring about the death of his term."[4]

Wasn't Reagan's and Bush's homophobic neglect of gay citizens afflicted by AIDS a form of anger? Those who denounce anger in politics are its most skilled practitioners, whose anger is apocalyptic in intensity and indiscriminate in its object. The louder their criticisms, the greater their responsibility. How else to explain the Republican Party officials' antipathy in the 1980s toward gay people they never met and who they let die without any remorse? At least ACT UP was selectively focused upon elected officials and agencies that were complicit. And they were honest about what was happening. Expressing anger concretely is better than being consumed by it. Let it out.

18

EMBRACE INTERCONNECTEDNESS

Disaster is often addressed piecemeal. Experts are convened to enact the smallest and most precise of interventions. After Hurricane Katrina devastated New Orleans in August 2005, the US Army Corps of Engineers was brought in to recommend fortifications for the city's failed levee system. After the Deepwater Horizon drilling rig exploded in 2010 in the Gulf of Mexico, and continued spilling for eighty-five days, its owner, the oil and gas behemoth BP, developed a cap to plug up an oil leak.

Such targeted and incremental change is also the response to the larger disaster of climate change, which Katrina was a product of and which the BP oil spill exacerbated. Recall that in the early 2000s, carbon credits—government-issued permits that allowed all corporations to emit greenhouse gases up to a certain point, popularized by former Democratic vice president

Al Gore—were in vogue as the best market incentive for big polluters to minimize their carbon footprint. Today, futuristic carbon-sucking machines that turn greenhouse gas into usable fertilizer are fashionable. Should we ban plastic straws or recycle more? Compost or reuse? Plant more trees or clean up trash in our neighborhoods?

None of these solutions come close to the scale of intervention needed to avoid further catastrophe. Bold, large-scale revolutionary thinking is urgently needed as the earth becomes more uninhabitable. When you think boldly, remember that everything is interconnected. Environmental justice is racial justice is economic justice is gender justice. Nonhuman life matters too. Dwindling in size and diversity, nearing extinction and finding itself plundered, sentient beings must also be saved from ever-expanding global capitalism that puts obscene profits above all else.

This was one message of the radical environmental movement in the 1980s. After years of pushing for meager reforms, they were exhausted by the snail's pace with which mainstream environmentalists lobbied congressmembers during business lunches on Capitol Hill. Radical environmentalists Dave Foreman, Ron Kezar, Bart Koehler, Mike Roselle, and Howie Wolke spent a week in the Pincate Desert of Northern Mexico to discuss mounting a militant response to wilderness degradation. By the end of the week, Earth First! was born. Without question, Earth First!ers were emboldened by what came before them. The Sierra Club, fresh from its success of preventing dams from being built in the Grand Canyon in 1968, organized Earth Day on April 22, 1970. In the 1980s, it protected 157 million acres of public lands in Alaska from oil drilling and stopped Reagan from dismantling the Clean Air Act. But these victories, Earth First! insisted, were nothing against the might of industrial capitalism, which continued slaughtering billions of animals for mass consumption yearly, fired up coal plants in major cities, and axed Pacific Northwest forests. This led to an unprecedented increase in dirty greenhouse gases that made global temperatures rise.

Unlike other national lobbying organizations like Friends of the Earth or the Wilderness Society, which were growing in ranks, Earth First! didn't start national chapters or furnish corporate offices. Instead, they sabotaged environmental destruction through wild acts of civil disobedience. "I think that the basic problem," Foreman later wrote, "goes beyond merely the question of whether violence (directed against either machines or people) is justified in protecting the earth. The real question is that of radicalizing the environmental movement."[1] Foreman's view caught on among young activists who, in April 1983, descended upon Bald Mountain in Idaho to block the construction of a road. Some stood with arms linked to prevent bulldozers from digging the earth. Others chained themselves to heavy machinery. Now construction crews couldn't dig as efficiently and quickly as they wanted. Another widely used tactic was the tree sit. In 1985, professional rock climbers ascended trees in an old-growth forest in Oregon's Willamette National Forest to force loggers to take human lives if they were willing to cut down majestic Douglas firs. A less visible but more controversial move to discourage logging in Northern California in the late 1980s was tree spiking, in which large nails were driven into trees. The US Forest Service and logging companies were notified about which trees were spiked and, so, had to choose whether to risk cutting them down and damaging their chainsaws. Their profit incentive had to be assessed against the potential of flying shards of metal that could injure their workers and destroy large, expensive machines.

These tactics aren't for everyone. You may question their efficacy. But Earth First!'s suspicion of anthropocentrism is undeniably important for this reason: placing human and nonhuman life on equal moral footing makes you critical of hierarchy. "Wilderness says: Human beings are not dominant," Foreman said. "Earth is not for *Homo sapiens* alone, human life is but one life form on the planet and has no right to take exclusive possession."[2] When you begin to think like this, you can't as readily buy into the tired arguments. Progress. Economic development. Globalization. A food chain is natural. The earth is to be plundered. Other nations are doing it; we should too.

Equipped with Earth First!'s ecocentrism, you think about social injustice. But as with most political philosophies, when taken to the extreme of devaluing human life and treating social injustice with apathy for the sake of wilderness preservation, it can be reactionary. This is what the radical environmentalist Murray Bookchin said about Earth First! in his 1987 address at the National Green Gathering in Amherst, Massachusetts, when he denounced elements of the movement as "barely disguised racists, survivalists, macho Daniel Boones."[3] Bookchin was correct. How else to explain a 1986 interview in which Foreman advocated immigration restriction on the US-Mexico border? As Foreman said, migrants put "more pressure on the resources we have in the USA" and bring an "alien mode of life which . . . is not appealing to the majority of Americans." Another article in the *Earth First! Journal* was explicitly homophobic in arguing that AIDS, given its destructiveness, could successfully lower the population and "industrialism, which is the main force behind the environmental crisis."[4]

Such rhetoric isn't just ugly. It's puzzling. If anything, it's a betrayal of Earth First!'s greatest insight: the critique of hierarchy. All movements can forget their roots. But luckily, there are always some who remember them. The anti-racist ecofeminist Judi Bari didn't want Earth First! to be sabotaged by misogynistic racists. So, as she became one of the organization's most visible figures, she explicitly advocated for "the feminization of" Earth First! Bari elevated women to leadership campaigns in her local chapter in California, and she equated the capitalist assault on nature with the misogyny of patriarchy. Under Bari's leadership, tree spiking, which began to draw incredible amounts of negative publicity and was routinely described by the media as ecoterrorism, was abandoned in favor of civil disobedience. Bari created common cause with timber workers, whom she didn't see as enemies but as people looking to feed their families while trapped in a capitalist system.

She also started a local chapter of the IWW union affiliated with Earth First! But being in the spotlight and advocating for reform aren't easy. They put you in the crosshairs of those who perceive you as an existential threat. On May 24, 1990, as Bari was driving her Subaru station wagon with a fellow activist, Darryl Cherney, from Oakland to Berkeley, an eleven-inch pipe bomb exploded under her seat, nearly killing her. It's still unclear who planted it. The government or disgruntled Earth First!ers? In the aftermath, the FBI took over the crime scene as part of a counter-terrorism investigation, alleging that Bari and Cherney were transporting explosives. This, as you can see, was an effective strategy to undermine the environmental movement by affiliating it with violence. Ultimately, however, neither Bari nor Cherney was charged with a crime.

Bari, having survived the FBI smear campaign and the assassination attempt, died seven years later from breast cancer in 1997, at the age of forty-seven. You see the ghost of Bari and Earth First! in advocates of the Green New Deal, which is about transitioning the US energy economy to clean, renewable sources. This means dismantling the fossil fuel industry. You see Bari in Extinction Rebellion, which was founded in the UK in 2018 but has since spread globally. Extinction

Rebellion's tactic of occupation and its decentralized network is meant to bring awareness to what it describes as the sixth mass extinction. Activists block traffic, stage die-ins, and lay down together in the Rockefeller Center ice rink, positioning their bodies to form the movement's emblem, an extinction symbol, which features two facing triangles within a circle. It's a performance and an attack on institutions, shaking citizens awake to do something. Now!

19

EMBRACE PARTICIPATORY DEMOCRACY

Economic inequality is one of the greatest disasters afflicting Americans today. According to Pew Research, the top 20 percent of American earners made more than half of all income in 2018. Between 1989 and 2016, the wealth gap between the richest and poorest more than doubled.[1] Nothing symbolizes this disparity more than the Great Recession of 2008, which was a culmination of thirty years of oligarchic rule marked by the privatization of public goods and the deregulation of the financial industry. Big banks like Goldman Sachs, J. P. Morgan Chase, Citigroup, and Wells Fargo were bailed out by the US Treasury Department. They were given a slap on the wrist with fines that did little to deter their bad behavior. Sincere public apologies were demanded of their executives, many of whom who got to keep their stock options and million-dollar yearly bonuses. Working Americans, in contrast, lost their life savings. Their retirement accounts plummeted. They were evicted from their homes.

To add insult to injury, working Americans were singled out as the primary culprits of the recession. The cause, according to leaders who themselves had been busy for years building up the real estate bubble, was working Americans' imprudence. They had made bad financial choices by taking on burdensome subprime mortgages they couldn't pay back. It wasn't the fault of the greedy banks, who pushed these mortgages and turned massive profits as a result of selling them. In the words of the billionaire New York mayor Michael Bloomberg, one of the richest people in the world, "What happened here is a bunch of people who didn't really have the wherewithal to get mortgages, got mortgages."[2]

What a predictable tactic. After disaster, you blame the disenfranchised, saying that the problem isn't that they were unjustly manipulated. You say that the marginal opportunities they received were, in fact, the cause of their undoing. When you make this sort of argument, you can even proclaim, as Bloomberg did at Georgetown University in September 2008, that the

Fair Housing Act of 1968's ban on the racist practice of redlining is responsible for the financial crisis.

The end to racial segregation, in which banks denied Black families mortgages because they were deemed "high risk," was, for Bloomberg, the real cause of our troubles. "Redlining, if you remember, was the term where banks took whole neighborhoods and said, 'People in these neighborhoods are poor, they're not going to be able to pay off their mortgages, tell your salesmen don't go into those areas.'" So, Bloomberg continued, "banks started making more and more loans where the credit of the person buying the house wasn't as good as you would like."[3]

Bloomberg's argument makes sense if you assume that our existing system of mortgage lending is fundamentally correct, that big banks should decide who to make loans to in a society where the free market rules supreme. However, if you don't agree, if you believe that housing is a right and that government should place limits on how much banks can profit from homeownership, then not only is Bloomberg's view dismantled, but you've now embraced a new idea of democracy. This new idea is that democracy can't be ruled by an oligarchic minority of the wealthy. It must be a participatory democracy in which power is shared among the majority of people, who get to decide how to spread the wealth they create.

This is what happened in the fall of 2011, during Bloomberg's third and final term as New York's mayor. It was then when a Canadian magazine, *Adbusters*, put out an ad that featured a ballerina perfectly balancing one foot on the iconic seven-thousand-pound bronze sculpture *Charging Bull* in New York's financial district. The headline read: "What Is Our One Demand? #OccupyWallStreet September 17. Bring a Tent." That day, hundreds of tents, carried by thousands of people, were brought to Zuccotti Park in the financial district. Their gathering would mark one of the most memorable experiments of direct democracy of late. Zuccotti Park, a privately owned space that doubles as a walkable park because a private developer wanted to erect private buildings in exchange for maintaining it, became a public festival. People from all over New York, and then from across the nation and the world, gathered to discuss revolutionary politics. They sang protest ballads, ate communal meals, made art, and read books.

Before being forcefully evicted by the NYPD six weeks later, in November 2011, Occupy Wall Street did something that we haven't seen since the 1960s. They explained to the general public how the financial crisis, and the government bailout that followed, was a product of a world in which the "1 percent" of the rich wielded far more influence than the "99 percent." If this was the argument Occupiers made about the ills of US democracy, then Zuccotti Park was their stage for embodying an alternative. The occupation created its own rules. Trash was picked up, and fiery debates were adjudicated through peaceful mediations. This happened without police intervention. Because New York City wouldn't allow loudspeakers, Occupiers resorted to an ingenious solution, what they called the "human megaphone," in which word of mouth was used to convey messages from the front of the crowd to the back. Collective decisions were reached through consensus rather than decree. The openness of the square allowed for the community to always change, from one minute to the next. The space wasn't enclosed and was visible to pedestrians who were on their way to work, to school, or enjoying a stroll in the neighborhood. There was no executive council of charismatic elites. No formal constitution or written rules. Not surprisingly, mainstream coverage of the movement, in the *New York Times* and *Washington Post*, construed this as a failure. What was Occupy's agenda or its concrete demands? What, beyond the spectacle and the tax and housing policies, did it want?

True, successful social movements affect change. But sometimes the measure of success isn't a specific proposal but, rather, how it inspires a future legacy. Who was inspired by Occupy's participatory democratic vision? A year later, in 2012, Black Lives Matter activists took to the streets against anti-Black racism after the brutal murder of a seventeen-year-old Black teen carrying Skittles in a gated community, Trayvon Martin, by a neighborhood watchman in Florida. In 2016, the Lakota at Standing Rock put their bodies on the line to prevent an oil pipeline from being built on their sacred land. The insurgent candidacy of the democratic socialist Vermont senator Bernie Sanders, in 2016, who openly spoke of the need for political revolution. His presidential runs that year and in 2020 were fueled by Occupy veterans. The Debt Collective, whose slogan is "You Are Not A Loan," and whose mission is to cancel exorbitant debt that weighs on a sizeable percentage of Americans, is on the front line petitioning the Biden administration to end $1.7 trillion of federal student-loan debt. Grassroots activism. Disruption, but not the kind embraced by Silicon Valley and Big Tech. Bodies in motion. This is what all such movements share, so that we can all share the world. We owe them all a debt, the kind they'd be okay with, but a debt that can't be monetized: the debt of gratitude.

20

THINK HISTORICALLY

The year 2020 was a hard one for most of us. But it was a banner year for disaster profiteers, who wanted to remake our world in their image. The New York governor, Democrat Andrew Cuomo, was praised by the national media early on for his cool-headed stewardship of the state's pandemic response in the spring. Unlike Trump, he held daily press conferences and took questions from reporters about daily infection and death rates related to the COVID-19 pandemic. It's good to keep the public informed. But not to use their goodwill to push for policies that would, in the long run, do damage to the common good. Cuomo, a fiscal moderate and longtime champion of lean government—dating back to his years as President Bill Clinton's Housing and Urban Development secretary in 1997 and then as New York's sixty-fourth attorney general—seized the economic crisis to cut necessary programs for the poorest

New Yorkers. Using an unprecedented drop in tax revenue and the lack of federal support as his overarching justification, Cuomo's 2021 budget plan called for 5 percent cuts to education, social services, and transportation, a $15 million cut for local homeless programs, and a $35 million reduction in state aid to community colleges.[1] If New York would only receive $6 billion from the federal government in COVID-related bailout aid, Cuomo explained, it was his intention to cut $2 billion in school funding, $600 million in Medicaid, and $900 million across the board.

When Cuomo came under attack from progressive critics, he retorted that the ultra-wealthy, too, would have to sacrifice. To be sure, the tax hike Cuomo proposed wasn't exactly burdensome. New Yorkers with incomes of more than $10 million would see their yearly rate inch up from 8.82 to 9.32 percent. And those making $100 million would have to pay a rate of 10.82 percent. But Cuomo wasn't done with wanting to shake things up. As it became clear early in April 2020 that public schools would shutter their doors and transition to online learning, Cuomo enlisted the help of the Bill and Melinda Gates Foundation and a former Google CEO, whom he described as "visionaries," to "reimagine" and "revolutionize" public education.[2] New York

State United Teachers, which boasts a membership of six hundred thousand, went to the heart of the matter in a blistering critique. Why, they asked, would the governor outsource the precious task of public education to billionaires whose stock-in-trade is profit-making and cost-cutting, rather than teaching young people? Why wouldn't Cuomo, they wondered, make New York a leader in greater federal funding for "social workers, mental health counselors, school nurses, enriching arts courses, advanced courses and smaller class sizes in school districts across the state?"[3]

Their pleas fell on deaf ears.

But if New York was ground zero for champions of privatization, state legislatures across the nation became a breeding ground for the enemies of representative government. After Trump didn't concede his seven-million-vote loss in the 2020 presidential election and began tweeting blatant lies about voter fraud on an hourly basis, as well as having his allies file dozens of frivolous lawsuits to try to overturn the election in the courts, Republicans recognized a plum opportunity to do what they've been doing for years: restrict the franchise.

The year 2020 saw the highest level of participation in a presidential election ever—158 million ballots were cast nationwide—partly because COVID-19 pushed states to expand eligibility for no-reason absentee, mail-in, and early voting. Republican state legislators across the nation saw the writing on the wall. And they weren't happy. By January 2021, they had filed a total of 106 bills to make voting harder—triple the number of similar bills the year before. In Georgia, for instance, they rolled back no-excuse absentee voting. And in Maricopa County, Arizona, a heavily Democratic district, they subpoenaed vote-tabulation equipment to scrutinize its use in future elections.

Brian Robinson, a Republican political consultant in Atlanta, says, "The overall purpose of these reforms is to restore faith in our election systems. . . . That's not to say that [the 2020 election] was a giant failure; that's to say that faith has been diminished."[4] Carefully scrutinize this logic: Republican voters believe there's voter fraud, though that is unsupported by any empirical evidence. They take this lie of fraud at face value, and in doing so support politicians who make it harder to vote for other citizens who don't support their policies. Democracy is hanging on life support with all the various voter-suppression efforts that Republicans have been putting in place for decades. Strict voter-ID laws, the closing of polling places, signature-matching requirements. Then, they say, let's double down! What's stunning isn't Republicans wanting to win by any means necessary. It's the brazenness with which they think they can justify it.

History has a funny way of repeating itself. But historical consciousness helps you fight back. As the Republican vote suppressors are emboldened again today, remember that southern white supremacists in the aftermath of the US Civil War in the 1890s came up with whatever lies they needed—Black people were stuffing ballot boxes, or were engaged in widespread political corruption—to roll back civil rights. Election officials required literacy tests and poll taxes that all but killed the Fifteenth Amendment's guarantee that formerly enslaved men had the right to vote.

Every disaster feels new. But it never is. Compare Hurricane Katrina destroying the Gulf Coast city of New Orleans in 2005 to Hurricane Maria eviscerating Puerto Rico in 2017. These were two different storms, twelve years apart. But that's where the difference ends. If anything, the parallels are eerie, if not predictable. There's the shocking apathy with which the Republican administration in power, Bush in 2005, Trump in 2017, responded. Then there's the rush to use public debt as leverage for privatizing everything in sight and pushing steep cuts to social services, meager to begin with. The absence of basic resources like water, food, and electricity for unimaginably long periods of time, for ordinary citizens. And the fortification of segregated ultra-rich communities, who, unlike the poor, have unlimited cash to meet all their needs, and much more.

Now that we're on the other side of the Trump presidency, it's the right time to reflect carefully about the state of our nation. After years of being bombarded by media coverage of the Trump years as somehow being outside of history—his presidency was norm-breaking, unlike anything we've seen in modern history, and so on—we've become desensitized to a long view of things. We're never living through an unprecedented moment. This is the final lesson of this book. Think historically. And be vigilant about the presence of the past. It's there, even if you can't see it. Remember how, after COVID hit, many headlines were pushing the same narrative? The pandemic will change everything forever! We'll be living in a brave new world! There will be a new normal!

Now ask yourself, today, how much, exactly, has fundamentally changed? Yes, hundreds of thousands of people lost their lives. Many of them for no other reason than the grotesque malfeasance of the Trump administration. But so much has remained the same. Inequality is as persistent as ever before: Racism. Xenophobia. Sexism. Homophobia. Climate change. Gun violence. Political corruption. Republicans still hold the poor in contempt and flirt with white nationalism. Democrats still yearn for bipartisanship and cozy up to big corporations who fund their reelection campaigns. Yes, there are more virtual meetings, and people continue to wear face masks. But the deep structures, which have been in place for decades, are still there. Unfortunately.

But there is one major difference between now and when COVID first hit. Today we have a historical archive of resistance since the pandemic began. Think of the nurses striking against bad working conditions in overcrowded hospitals. Black Lives Matter describing racism as a pandemic that has afflicted the US for four hundred years. Amazon workers attempting to unionize in Alabama. Public school teachers in Chicago and New York refusing to return to overcrowded and poorly ventilated schools. Forget, for a minute, about who's president. Or the latest disaster we just experienced. Resistance is there. Somewhere. Even if you can't see it. Just as it's been there since the beginning of US history.

Let this anchor you in dark times. When the next disaster strikes—and it will, tomorrow, a month from now, or five years from now—be ready. Breathe. Compose yourself. Slow things down. You'll be told that there's only one realistic way to do things. That if you don't do it this way or that way, you're immature. Irrational. Silly. Naïve. They're wrong. The historical record is in plain sight. Of freedom fighters who didn't profit from disaster. Who courageously risked their safety so others wouldn't die by it. Yes, disasters, big and small, will persist. Count on it. But your response matters. Will you be paralyzed by fear, or find solidarity with strangers? Will you organize, or suffer alone? Will you bear witness, or shut your eyes? Express righteous indignation, or wither away in silence? Settle for the possible, or demand the impossible?

In the words of the great American writer James Baldwin, "Not everything that is faced can be changed, but nothing can be changed until it is faced."[5] Keep these prophetic words in mind. If you do, when you face the next American disaster, the world will become both smaller and larger. Smaller because you know what can be done today. Larger because something new is possible tomorrow.

ACKNOWLEDGMENTS

Thank you to my editor at Beacon, Rachael Marks, for her suggestions and for her ongoing support of my work; to Susan Lumenello, for astute copyediting; to the entire Beacon team, who are a treasure in the publishing world. Thanks, too, to my literary agent, Matthew Carnicelli, for his relentless enthusiasm. Thanks to my friends, family, and colleagues and students at the University of Detroit Mercy. And, as ever, thank you to my children, Sam and Anita, and to my partner, Alison Powell.

NOTES

1. DISASTERS ARE OPPORTUNITIES

1. Rahm Emanuel, "Let's Make Sure This Crisis Doesn't Go to Waste," *Washington Post*, March 25, 2020.

2. Edward McClelland, "Why Rahm Can't Shake Reaganism," *Chicago Magazine*, August 27, 2020, https://www.chicagomag.com/news/august-2020/why-rahm-cant-shake-reaganism.

3. Milton Friedman, *Capitalism and Freedom: Fortieth Anniversary Edition* (Chicago: University of Chicago Press, 2002), xiv.

4. Ian Schwartz, "Rahm Emanuel: Pay People Who Lost Retail Jobs to 'Become a Computer Coder,'" *RealClearPolitics*, November 7, 2020, https://www.realclearpolitics.com/video/2020/11/07/rahm_emanuel_pay_people_who_lost_retail_jobs_to_become_a_computer_coder.html.

2. RESIST

1. John F. Harris and Sarah Zimmerman, "Trump May Not Be Crazy, but the Rest of Us Are Getting There Fast," *Politico*,

October 12, 2018, https://www.politico.com/magazine/story /2018/10/12/donald-trump-anxiety-disorder-pscyhologists -221305.

2. Mychal Denzel Smith, "A Biden Win Won't Cure My Trump-Era Depression," *New York Times*, September 11, 2020, https://www.nytimes.com/2020/09/11/opinion/trump-biden -2020-depression.html.

3. Roxanne Dunbar-Ortiz, *An Indigenous Peoples' History of the United States* (Boston: Beacon Press, 2015), 26.

4. Howard Zinn, *A People's History of the United States* (New York: Harper, 2015), 20.

3. TAKE BACK THE STREETS

1. The best account of this is in Peter Linebaugh and Markus Rediker, *The Many-Headed Hydra: Sailors, Slaves, Commoners, and the Hidden History of the Revolutionary Atlantic* (Boston: Beacon Press, 2013).

2. Linebaugh and Rediker, *The Many-Headed Hydra*, 216.

3. Thomas Jefferson, "Letter to Abigail Adams," February 22, 1787, https://founders.archives.gov/documents/Adams /04–07–02–0187.

4. Julia Reinstein, "The Woman in 'Lose Yo Job' Video Told Us How It Changed Her Life," *Buzzfeed*, June 8, 2020, https://www.buzzfeednews.com/article/juliareinstein/lose -yo-job-viral-video-woman-johnniqua-charles.

4. PATRIOTISM ISN'T THE ANSWER

1. Geoffrey Plank, *John Woolman's Path to the Peaceable Kingdom: A Quaker in the British Empire* (Philadelphia: University of Pennsylvania Press, 2012), 133.

2. Plank, *John Woolman's Path to the Peaceable Kingdom*, 152.

3. Plank, *John Woolman's Path to the Peaceable Kingdom*, 203.

4. Plank, *John Woolman's Path to the Peaceable Kingdom*, 173.

5. REDEFINE IDEALS TO MEET YOUR DEMOCRATIC ASPIRATIONS

1. Brian Naylor, "Read Trump's Jan. 6 Speech, a Key Part of Impeachment Trial," February 6, 2021, NPR, https://www
.npr.org/2021/02/10/966396848/read-trumps-jan-6-speech
-a-key-part-of-impeachment-trial.

2. Billy House, "McCarthy Opposes Impeachment, Privately Floats Other Responses," *Bloomberg*, January 11, 2021,
https://www.bloomberg.com/news/articles/2021-01-11
/mccarthy-tells-gop-colleagues-he-opposes-trump-s
-impeachment.

3. Donald Nielson, "The Mashpee Indian Revolt of 1833,"
New England Quarterly 58, no. 3 (September 1985): 400–420.

4. Daniel Mandell, "We, as a Tribe, Will Rule Ourselves:
Mashpee's Struggle for Autonomy, 1746–1840," *Colonial Society of Massachusetts* 71 (2003), https://www.colonialsociety.org
/node/1407#ren548, accessed August 20, 2021.

5. Elizabeth Cady Stanton, "Declaration of Sentiments,"
available at National Park Service, https://www.nps.gov/wori
/learn/historyculture/declaration-of-sentiments.htm.

6. Frederick Douglass, "What to a Slave Is the Fourth of
July?" *Nation*, July 4, 2012, https://www.thenation.com/article
/archive/what-slave-fourth-july-frederick-douglass.

6. POLITICIZE TRUTH

1. Katy Steinmetz, "How Your Brain Tricks You into Believing Fake News," *Time*, August 9, 2018, https://time.com
/5362183/the-real-fake-news-crisis; Kurt Anderson, "How
America Lost Its Mind," *The Atlantic*, September 2017,

https://www.theatlantic.com/magazine/archive/2017/09/how
-america-lost-its-mind/534231.

2. David W. Blight, "'For Something Beyond the Battlefield': Frederick Douglass and the Struggle for the Memory of
the Civil War," *Journal of American History* 75, no. 4 (March
1989): 1160.

3. Blight, "'For Something Beyond the Battlefield,'" 1163.

4. Blight, "'For Something Beyond the Battlefield,'" 1161.

5. Blight, "'For Something Beyond the Battlefield,'" 1169.

7. IMAGINE UTOPIA

1. Robert Owen, "A New View of Society," in *A New View
of Society and Other Writings* (New York: Penguin, 2019), 40.

2. Chris Jennings, *Paradise Now: The Story of American
Utopianism* (New York: Random House, 2017), 123.

3. Ralph Waldo Emerson, *Political Writings* (Cambridge:
Cambridge University Press, 2008), 117.

8. QUESTION ELITES

1. Vivian Gornick, *Emma Goldman: Revolution as a Way of
Life* (New Haven, CT: Yale University Press, 2011), 16.

2. Emma Goldman, *Anarchism and Other Essays* (New
York: Mother Earth Publishing, 1910), 65.

3. Goldman, *Anarchism and Other Essays*, 65.

4. Peter Marshall, *Demanding the Impossible: A History of
Anarchism* (Oakland, CA: PM Press, 2010), 398.

5. Gornick, *Emma Goldman*, 4.

9. MAKE PEACE

1. Michael Kazin, "America and the Great War," *Raritan* 32,
no. 1 (Summer 2004): 76.

2. Kazin, "America and the Great War," 77.

3. Jane Addams, *Peace and Bread in Time of War* (New York: MacMillan, 1922), 142.

4. Roger Baldwin, "Conscience at the Bar," *The Survey* 41 (October 1918–March 1919): 154.

5. Kazin, "America and the Great War," 83.

10. BUILD A DEMOCRATIC SOCIETY

1. Joe Garofoli, "Biden Promises a Return to Normalcy: Is America Ready to Go There?," *SF Chronicle*, January 20, 2021, https://www.sfchronicle.com/politics/article/Biden-promises-a-return-to-normalcy-Is-America-15883179.php.

2. Philip A. Cusick, *A Passion for Learning: The Education of Seven Eminent Americans* (New York: Teachers College Press, 2005), 150.

3. Roger Lee Ray, *Progressive Faith and Practice: Thou Shalt Not Stand Idly By* (Eugene, OR: Wipf and Stock, 2014), 116.

4. Dorothy Day, *The Commonweal* 55, Issues 13–26 (Berkeley: University of California Press, 1952), 637.

5. Gary Dorrien, *Social Ethics in the Making: Interpreting an American Tradition* (London: Wiley, 2011), 375.

11. ORGANIZE

1. Eugene Debs, "Speech of Acceptance," *International Socialist Review* (October 1912).

12. MAKE POLITICAL ART

1. "What's in President Trump's Fiscal 2021 Budget?," *New York Times*, February 10, 2020, https://www.nytimes.com/2020/02/10/business/economy/trump-budget-explained-facts.html.

2. Morris Dickstein, *Dancing in the Dark: A Cultural History of the Great Depression* (New York: Norton, 2009), 23.

3. Michael Gold, *Jews Without Money* (New York: Public Affairs, 2004), 311.

4. "I Aimed for the Public's Heart and . . . Hit It in the Stomach, *Chicago Tribune*, May 21, 2006, https://www.chicagotribune.com/news/ct-xpm-2006–05–21–0605210414-story.html.

5. Linda Gordon, "Dorothea Lange: The Photographer as Agricultural Sociologist," *Journal of American History* 93, no. 3 (2006): 705.

6. Richard Wright, *12 Million Black Voices* (New York: Basic Books, 2002), 146.

13. PAINT A BLOODY PICTURE

1. John Hersey, "Hiroshima," *New Yorker*, August 31, 1946, https://www.newyorker.com/magazine/1946/08/31/hiroshima.

2. Hersey, "Hiroshima."

3. Stefanie Glinski, "Afghan Families Torn Apart by Drone Strikes," *Guardian*, December 6, 2019, https://www.theguardian.com/news/2019/dec/06/afghan-families-torn-apart-drone-strikes-picture-essay.

4. Heather Stringer, "Psychologists Respond to Mental Health Crisis at the Border," American Psychological Association, July 2018, https://www.apa.org/news/apa2018/border-family-separation.

14. POLITICIZE GRIEF

1. Brittany Bernstein, "Kamala Harris Told Jacob Blake She Was 'Proud' of Him, Lawyer Says," *Yahoo! News*, September 8, 2020, https://news.yahoo.com/kamala-harris-told-jacob-blake-130728218.html.

2. Mamie Till-Mobley and Christopher Bensen, *Death of Innocence: The Story of the Hate Crime That Changed America* (New York: One World, 2003), 135.

3. Till-Mobley and Bensen, *Death of Innocence*, 139.

4. Devery Anderson, *Emmett Till: The Murder That Shocked the World and Propelled the Civil Rights Movement* (Jackson: University Press of Mississippi, 2015), 251.

5. Barack Obama, "Remarks by the President in Eulogy for the Honorable Reverend Clementa Pinckney," College of Charleston, June 26, 2015, https://obamawhitehouse.archives .gov/the-press-office/2015/06/26/remarks-president-eulogy -honorable-reverend-clementa-pinckney.

16. REVOLUTIONIZE IDENTITY

1. Yuki Noguchi, "For Many #MeToo Accusers, Speaking Up Is Just the Beginning," NPR, November 5, 2019, https:// www.npr.org/2019/11/05/772223109/for-many-metoo-accusers -speaking-up-is-just-the-beginning.

2. Alex Press, "Women Are Filing More Harassment Claims in the #MeToo Era. They're Also Facing More Retaliation," *Vox*, May 9, 2019, https://www.vox.com/the-big-idea/2019/5/9 /18541982/sexual-harassment-me-too-eeoc-complaints.

3. Nona Willis Aronowitz, "The First Time Women Shouted Their Abortions," *New York Times*, March 23, 2019, https://www .nytimes.com/2019/03/23/opinion/sunday/abortion-speakout -anniversary.html.

4. Michael Bronski, *A Queer History of the United States* (Boston: Beacon Press, 2012), 210.

5. Jennifer Nelson, *Women of Color and the Reproductive Rights Movement* (New York: New York University Press, 2003), 69.

6. Nelson, *Women of Color and the Reproductive Rights Movement*, 66.

7. Nelson, *Women of Color and the Reproductive Rights Movement*, 65.

17. MAKE AN ANGRY SPECTACLE

1. Steven Webster, "Angry Americans: How Political Rage Helps Campaigns but Hurts Democracy," *The Conversation*, https://theconversation.com/angry-americans-how-political -rage-helps-campaigns-but-hurts-democracy-145819.

2. German Lopez, "The Reagan Administration's Unbeliev- able Response to the HIV/AIDS Epidemic," *Vox*, December 1, 2016, https://www.vox.com/2015/12/1/9828348/ronald-reagan -hiv-aids.

3. Deborah Gould, *Moving Politics: ACT UP's Fight Against AIDS* (Chicago: University of Chicago Press, 2009), 226.

4. Phillip Picardi, "'George Bush, Serial Killer': ACT UP's Fight Against the President," *Out*, December 1, 2018, https:// www.out.com/out-exclusives/2018/12/01/george-bush-serial -killer-act-ups-fight-against-president.

18. EMBRACE INTERCONNECTEDNESS

1. Keith Makoto Woodhouse, *The Ecocentrists: A History of Radical Environmentalism* (New York: Columbia University Press, 2018), 133.

2. James Sterba, *Earth Ethics: Environmental Ethics, An- imal Rights, and Practical Applications* (New York: Prentice Hall, 1995), 348.

3. Woodhouse, *The Ecocentrists*, 195.

4. Woodhouse, *The Ecocentrists*, 196.

19. EMBRACE PARTICIPATORY DEMOCRACY

1. Katherine Schaeffer, "6 Facts About Economic Inequality in the United States," Pew Research, February 7, 2020, https://www.pewresearch.org/fact-tank/2020/02/07/6-facts-about-economic-inequality-in-the-u-s.

2. Sarah Jones, "Bloomberg Repeatedly Blamed Homeowners for the Recession," *New York Magazine*, March 2, 2020, https://nymag.com/intelligencer/2020/03/bloomberg-absolved-banks-blamed-homeowners-for-recession.html.

3. Jones, "Bloomberg Repeatedly Blamed Homeowners for the Recession."

20. THINK HISTORICALLY

1. Tom Precious, "Jobs and Services in Jeopardy If Cuomo Budget Cuts Stand and Federal Money Doesn't Come," *Buffalo News*, January 21, 2021, https://buffalonews.com/news/state-and-regional/govt-and-politics/jobs-and-services-in-jeopardy-if-cuomo-budget-cuts-stand-and-federal-money-doesnt-come/article_0912654e-5c10–11eb-9664-cfebaa3e9fc7.html.

2. Theodore Schleifer, "Andrew Cuomo Is Leaning on Tech Billionaires to Help New York Rebuild," *Vox*, May 6, 2020, https://www.vox.com/recode/2020/5/6/21249410/coronavirus-andrew-cuomo-bill-gates-eric-schmidt-tech-billionaires.

3. Diane Rutherford, "Teachers Union, Education Advocates Voice Concerns as Cuomo Looks to 'Reimagine' Education," *7 News*, May 5, 2020, https://www.wwnytv.com/2020/05/05/teachers-union-education-advocates-voice-concerns-cuomo-looks-reimagine-education.

4. Michael Wines, "After Record Turnout, Republicans Are Trying to Make It Harder to Vote," *New York Times*, January

30, 2021, https://www.nytimes.com/2021/01/30/us/republicans
-voting-georgia-arizona.html.

5. James Baldwin, "As Much Truth as One Can Bear; to
Speak Out About the World as It Is, Says James Baldwin, Is the
Writer's Job," *New York Times*, January 14, 1962, https://www
.nytimes.com/1962/01/14/archives/as-much-truth-as-one-can
-bear-to-speak-out-about-the-world-as-it-is.html.